An Introduction to John Owen

John Owen

"In the relatively brief compass of this fresh approach to the core intellectual ideas of John Owen, Crawford Gribben has written what amounts to a must-read work about the *mentalité* of this theological colossus. A fabulous achievement!"

Michael A. G. Haykin, Chair and Professor of Church History, The Southern Baptist Theological Seminary

"Studying John Owen's life and theology is like visiting a vast food buffet—delicious but overwhelming, resulting in satisfaction but also a sense that one missed quite a lot. Crawford Gribben serves up a sampler plate with an engaging blend of biography and doctrine flavored with the pervasive sauce of Owen's view of godliness and spiced with Gribben's own interpretation of Owen's story. This book is a helpful introduction to one of the greatest theologians our world has known and a healthy enticement to feed on Owen's writings for a lifetime."

Joel R. Beeke, President, Puritan Reformed Theological Seminary; author, *Reformed Preaching*; coauthor, *Reformed Systematic Theology*

"Crawford Gribben draws on expertise gathered over years of work on John Owen to paint a picture that is both deeply scholarly and extremely readable. Looking at different stages of human life through the prism of Owen's personal experience and theological writings, the book gives a striking new perspective on this significant Reformed theologian. It's an excellent introduction to Owen."

Susan Hardman Moore, Professor of Early Modern Religion, School of Divinity, University of Edinburgh; author, *Pilgrims: New World Settlers and the Call of Home*

"John Owen is one of the most remarkable figures to emerge out of seventeenth-century England. His writings span a wide range of topics, from Trinitarian theology and religious toleration to educational reform and personal piety. While recent scholarship has helped us reevaluate Owen in significant ways, a one-dimensional portrait of the Puritan often emerges, whether as a timeless theologian or as an outdated historical figure. Crawford Gribben's book excels at situating Owen's theology in the times in which he wrote. The result is not only a stimulating exercise in biographical theology but also a compelling vision of the Christian life. For those wanting to get to know Owen the man as well as Owen the theologian, this book is the best place to start."

John W. Tweeddale, Academic Dean and Professor of Theology, Reformation Bible College; author, *John Owen and Hebrews*

"This is a beautifully written book. It is accessible and uplifting, blending the highest scholarship with deep devotion. Gribben presents John Owen in a fresh new light. It has something for those who are new to Owen as well as for those who have read him for a lifetime. Gribben's introduction is an essential, life-giving guide to a great man whose influence is still with us."

Tim Cooper, Associate Professor of Church History, University of Otago, New Zealand; author, *John Owen, Richard Baxter, and the Formation of Nonconformity*

AN

INTRODUCTION

TO

JOHN
OWEN

A

CHRISTIAN VISION
FOR EVERY STAGE
OF LIFE

CRAWFORD GRIBBEN

WHEATON, ILLINOIS

An Introduction to John Owen: A Christian Vision for Every Stage of Life

Copyright © 2020 by Crawford Gribben

Published by Crossway
        1300 Crescent Street
        Wheaton, Illinois 60187

This book quotes from manuscript material in the possession of the Bodleian Library, Inspire Nottinghamshire Archives, and Dr. Williams's Library. Used by permission.

Portions of this book are drawn from Crawford Gribben, "John Owen (1616–1683): Four Centuries of Influence," *Reformation Today* 273 (September–October 2016): 10–18. Used by permission of *Reformation Today*.

Cover design: Jordan Eskovitz

Cover image: Portrait by John Greenhill, National Portrait Gallery, London.

First printing 2020

Printed in the United States of America

Scripture quotations are from the *King James Version* (KJV) of the Bible.

Trade paperback ISBN: 978-1-4335-6965-4
Epub ISBN: 978-1-4335-6968-5
PDF ISBN: 978-1-4335-6966-1
Mobipocket ISBN: 978-1-4335-6967-8

Library of Congress Cataloging-in-Publication Data

Names: Gribben, Crawford, author.
Title: An introduction to John Owen : a Christian vision for every stage of life / Crawford Gribben.
Description: Wheaton, Illinois : Crossway, 2020. | Includes bibliographical references and indexes.
Identifiers: LCCN 2019032178 (print) | LCCN 2019032179 (ebook) | ISBN 9781433569654 (trade paperback) | ISBN 9781433569661 (pdf) | ISBN 9781433569678 (mobi) | ISBN 9781433569685 (epub)
Subjects: LCSH: Owen, John, 1616–1683. | Spiritual life—Christianity. | Grace (Theology)
Classification: LCC BX5207.O88 G748 2020 (print) | LCC BX5207.O88 (ebook) | DDC 230/.59092—dc23
LC record available at https://lccn.loc.gov/2019032178
LC ebook record available at https://lccn.loc.gov/2019032179

Crossway is a publishing ministry of Good News Publishers.

VP   29   28   27   26   25   24   23   22   21   20
15   14   13   12   11   10   9   8   7   6   5   4   3   2   1

For Pauline, Daniel, Honor, Finn, and Samuel

Contents

Maps 10

Preface 13

Time Line 17

Bibliographic Note 23

Introduction 25

1   Childhood 47

2   Youth 71

3   Middle Age 91

4   Death and Eternal Life 117

Conclusion 143

Appendix 155
        Prayers for Children from John Owen, *The Primer* (1652)

Bibliography 159

General Index 183

Scripture Index 189

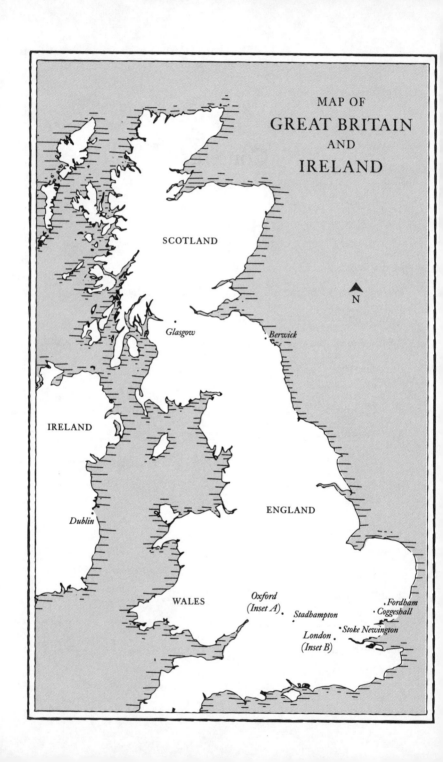

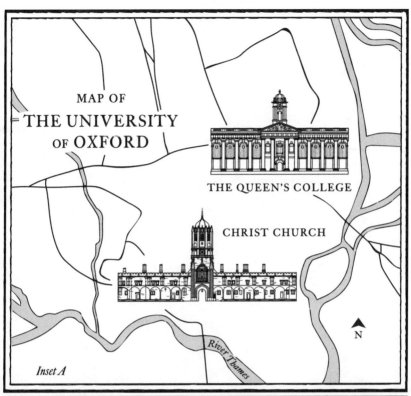

MAP OF
THE UNIVERSITY
OF OXFORD

THE QUEEN'S COLLEGE

CHRIST CHURCH

River Thames

N

Inset A

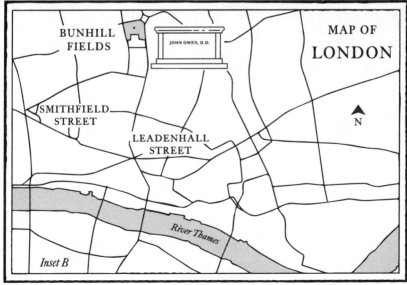

BUNHILL
FIELDS

JOHN OWEN, D.D.

MAP OF
LONDON

N

SMITHFIELD
STREET

LEADENHALL
STREET

River Thames

Inset B

Preface

John Owen (1616–1683) was the greatest—and certainly the most formidable—of English Protestant theologians. This book is an introduction to his work, but it is not an attempt at theological weight lifting. Instead, it is about Owen's description of the spiritual lives of his ideal readers. Its driving force is not Owen's biography, which I reconstructed in *John Owen and English Puritanism: Experiences of Defeat* (2016). Instead, it sets out to discover the kind of life he hoped his readers would experience. For Owen, spiritual life was about increasing in grace and goodness, in fellowship with each person of the Trinity, in the local and visible, catholic and invisible fellowship of the church, in the context of an often hostile world. Divine grace was always experienced in a social, cultural, and political context and made a contribution to it. The good life would be enabled by divine grace and would extend that grace to others.

I owe the idea for this approach to Carey Newman, who suggested to me that an introduction to Owen should do more than work through his responses to major debates in the Reformed tradition. After all, there already exists a great deal of historical-theological work in this field, and readers can find in the bibliography major expositions of most of the central themes in Owen's work. Much of this work is extremely valuable in understanding Owen's achievements. But this book sets out to do something new. If my work *John Owen and English Puritanism* was an exercise in theological biography, the present project might be regarded as an exercise in biographical theology. It considers the kind of Christian life that Owen wanted to promote, showing some of the unexpected ways in which he articulated his famously high Calvinism and how he expected it to play out in the lives of those he influenced. Its chapters discuss some of the best-known and least-known of Owen's works, which I have chosen to focus on as works that treat especially his concerns about the distinctive challenges of successive stages of the Christian life. From infancy to death—and beyond—Owen described the spiritual life as being sustained by and sustaining others in grace.

This book builds on, and occasionally modifies, more than two decades of reading and writing about Owen and his contexts. I first encountered Owen's works in the mid-1990s, during my doctoral studies, under the guidance of Michael Bath of the University of Strathclyde and Eiléan Ní Chuilleanáin of Trinity College Dublin. I have since published a biography of Owen, as well as a number of articles and chapters on his significance, and I've updated the conclusions of several of those works here. In the intervening years, my thinking about Owen has been stimulated by John Coffey, Tim Cooper, Sinclair Ferguson, Michael Haykin, and John Tweeddale, while my reading of early modern literature, history, and theology has been guided and informed by colleagues including Matt Bingham, Ian Campbell, Chris Caughey, R. Scott Clark, Martyn Cowan, Scott Dixon, Darryl Hart, Ariel Hessayon, Andrew Holmes, Neil Keeble, Richard Muller, Graeme Murdock, Amanda Piesse, Murray Pittock, Ian Campbell Ross, Nigel Smith, Scott Spurlock, Mark Sweetnam, and Joe Webster. I am grateful to

Michael Haykin to reuse material that I initially published in an issue of *Reformation Today*, which he edited, and to the Bodleian Library, Inspire Nottinghamshire Archives, and Dr. Williams's Library for permission to quote from manuscript material in their possession. Most important, my reading of Owen's work has been something I have shared with members of my family, who are "heirs together of the grace of life" and to whom this book is dedicated.

Owen understood that the "praise of God's grace . . . ought to be the end of all our Writing and Reading in this world."[1] This book describes Owen's suggestions as to how that grace should flow through the Christian life, from birth to the beatific vision, as the gift of the one who is the source, guide, and goal of all things: *Mar is uaidh agus is tríd agus is chuige atá gach ní dá bhfuil ann. Moladh go deo leis* (Rom. 11:36).

Crawford Gribben
Tulaigh na Mullán, December 2019

---

1. John Owen, "Dr. Owen to the Reader," in Henry Scudder, *The Christians Daily Walk* (London, 1674), sig. A2v.

Time Line

1616   Owen is born in Stadhampton, Oxfordshire.

1626   Owen enters Edward Sylvester's school, Oxford.

1628   Owen enters the Queen's College, Oxford.

1632   Owen graduates with a bachelor of arts and is ordained as a deacon by John Bancroft, bishop of Oxford.

1635   Owen graduates with a master of arts.

1637   Owen leaves Oxford without clear prospects for employment.

1638   Owen is ordained as a priest by John Bancroft, bishop of Oxford.

1641–1642   Owen acts as chaplain for Sir Robert Dormer of Ascot and John, Lord Lovelace of Hurley.

1642   With the outbreak of civil war, Owen leaves the Lovelace household, takes lodgings near Smithfield, London, and gains assurance of salvation under the preaching of an unknown minister.

1643   Owen publishes his first book, *A Display of Arminianism*, becomes minister of Fordham, Essex, and marries Mary Rooke.

1644   Owen's first son, John, is born.

1645   Owen publishes his two catechisms.

1646	Owen becomes minister of Coggeshall, Essex, and preaches to the House of Commons for the first time at the conclusion of the First Civil War.
1647	Owen's daughters Mary and Elizah die.
1648	Owen's son Thomas dies. The Second Civil War erupts, and Owen's attendance at and preaching after the siege of Colchester brings him to the attention of Thomas, Lord Fairfax; into the orbit of the army; and ultimately to the attention of Oliver Cromwell. Owen publishes *The Death of Death in the Death of Christ*.
1649	After the trial and execution of Charles I, England becomes a republic. Owen preaches to members of Parliament (MPs) on the day after the regicide and comes to national attention. Owen's only surviving child, John, dies. Owen meets Oliver Cromwell and joins his invasion of Ireland; he spends the autumn preaching and writing in Dublin, while the army subjugates the island in a series of controversial actions, and for the first time he notes that his ministry has been attended by conversions.
1650	Owen returns home to the birth of a daughter, Mary, who is by then his only living child, and almost immediately joins Cromwell's summer invasion of Scotland; he preaches in Berwick and debates with Presbyterians in Glasgow.
1651	Owen's daughter Elizabeth is born, and Owen is appointed as dean of Christ Church, University of Oxford.
1652	Owen preaches at the state funeral of Henry Ireton, Cromwell's son-in-law. He chairs the committee that reports on the errors of the Racovian Catechism and begins to define the theological boundaries of a national religious settlement in *The Humble Proposals*; he publishes *The Primer* and is appointed vice-chancellor of the University of Oxford.

1653   Owen's regular preaching in Oxford is recorded by students, including Thomas Aldersey.

1654   Owen becomes a "trier" and adjudicates which preachers should be supported by the state. He is noted as being out of sympathy with the increasingly conservative direction of the government of the republic; is elected as an MP to the first Protectoral Parliament, where he is associated with republican critics of the Cromwellian regime; but is almost immediately forced to resign his seat on account of his being ordained. Owen publishes *The Doctrine of the Saints' Perseverance.*

1655   Owen raises forces in Oxford to combat a royalist rising, publishes his anti-Socinian polemic *Vindiciae Evangelicae,* and takes part in discussion about the readmittance of the Jews.

1656   Two of Owen's sons, whose names are not recorded, die. Owen publishes *Of the Mortification of Sin in Believers.*

1657   Owen publishes *Of Communion with God.* Reflecting his increasing concern about the direction of government, he writes a statement on behalf of republican army officers to oppose the proposition that Cromwell should be offered the crown. Owen's term as vice-chancellor of the University of Oxford is not renewed, though his leadership of Christ Church continues.

1658   Owen publishes *Of Temptation,* several books on schism, and discussions of the nature of Scripture. Oliver Cromwell dies, and his son Richard succeeds him as Lord Protector. Owen and other Independents revise the Westminster Confession as a national statement of faith that becomes known as the Savoy Declaration. Owen walks in the procession attending Cromwell's funeral alongside other civil servants, including John Milton, Andrew Marvell, and John Dryden.

1659   Owen preaches his last sermon to MPs and gathers a congregation at Wallingford House, London, from which he coordinates responses of army republicans to increasing political chaos and fears of renewed civil war. Owen corresponds with George Monck, commander of the army in Scotland, who is marching south, about his intentions regarding the political settlement, but Monck plays for time while also communicating with the exiled king.

1660   Owen leaves Christ Church and returns to Stadhampton, where he gathers a church in his home. Monck's march south provokes panic in London, which is followed by desertions from the army in England, and so enables the return and restoration of Charles II. Owen is not listed among those to suffer exemplary punishment for their participation in the revolution, but some of his political and religious colleagues experience public deaths of extraordinary cruelty, following which their dismembered corpses are displayed around London.

1661   Uncertain of how to understand the sudden reversal of his hopes, Owen publishes *Theologoumena Pantodapa* and turns away from scholastic theology.

1662   After the Act of Uniformity, around 2,500 ministers leave the national church to become dissenters and to suffer under a series of laws that become known as the Clarendon Code. Trying to evade arrest, not always successfully, Owen and his wife live apart from their surviving children in the homes of several well-connected patrons. Owen publishes *Animadversions on a Treatise Intituled Fiat Lux*, which seems to reverse some of his previous commitments, and *A Discourse concerning Liturgies*, which restates them.

1664	Owen's daughter Judith dies. Owen gathers a church in the home of the Fleetwood family, in Stoke Newington, where Sir John Hartopp begins to take notes on his preaching.
1665–1666	The Great Plague, a major outbreak of the bubonic plague, kills around 25 percent of the population of London. Owen's son Matthew dies.
1666	The Great Fire of London devastates the housing of tens of thousands of the capital's inhabitants. Owen, like other dissenters, discerns God's providential judgment on his persecutors.
1667	Owen publishes pamphlets arguing for political liberties for dissenters and *A Brief Instruction in the Worship of God*.
1668	Owen publishes the first of several volumes of his commentary on Hebrews.
1669	Owen publishes his commentary on Psalm 130.
1672	Charles II issues a Declaration of Indulgence, which offers greater liberties to Protestant dissenters and Catholics but which is extremely controversial among supporters of the Church of England.
1673	Parliament forces Charles to withdraw the indulgence and imposes the first Test Act, which requires those taking part in public life to attend Communion in an Anglican church. Owen's small congregation, based around the Fleetwood family, joins with the much larger congregation that had been led by Joseph Caryl, who had recently died, and they gather in their premises on Leadenhall Street, London. Lucy Hutchinson and Sir John Hartopp take notes on Owen's preaching.
1674	Owen publishes *A Discourse concerning the Holy Spirit*.

1676	Owen publishes *The Nature of Apostasy*.
1677	Owen's first wife, Mary, dies. Owen publishes *The Doctrine of Justification*, helps secure the release from prison of John Bunyan, and marries Dorothy D'Oyley, a member of his congregation.
1681	Owen publishes *The Grace and Duty of Being Spiritually Minded*.
1682	Owen's last surviving child, Mary (b. 1650), dies.
1683	Owen declines in health, dies, and is buried in Bunhill Fields, London.

Bibliographic Note

The Works of John Owen, edited by William H. Goold, 24 volumes (Edinburgh: Johnstone and Hunter, 1850–1855), remains the standard edition of Owen's works. It has been almost entirely reprinted in facsimile as *The Works of John Owen*, edited by William H. Goold (1850–1855; repr., Edinburgh: Banner of Truth, 1965–1968), but the reprint edition does not contain Goold's volume 17, and it reorganizes the content of his volume 16. Nevertheless, throughout this book, I refer to the edition of *The Works of John Owen* that is kept in print by the Banner of Truth, which is the most widely available edition of Owen's works.

Introduction

By any account, John Owen (1616–1683) was extraordinary.[1] Not only was he one of the most learned, insightful, and influential English Puritan theologians, he was also one of the most important, and certainly one of the most voluminous, seventeenth-century writers. His eight million words were published in eighty separate titles and ranged from a short Latin poem in praise of Oliver Cromwell to the longest and one of the most technically demanding commentaries that has ever been published on the New Testament epistle to the Hebrews. Best known for his defense of high Calvinism, Owen wrote extensively in favor of religious toleration. Often regarded as a scholastic theologian, Owen cited classical writers, Geoffrey Chaucer, and Dante Alighieri to make theological points, while amassing one of the largest and most diverse private libraries of the seventeenth century and knowing and collecting the works of its best-known poets. While often ambitious to make his own mark, he facilitated the literary careers of other writers, including Andrew Marvell and John Bunyan. Austere and sometimes

---

1. This chapter develops a short biography that was published as Crawford Gribben, "John Owen: Four Centuries of Influence," *Reformation Today* 273 (September–October 2016), 10–18, with the permission of the editor. For a more complete biography, where sources for these arguments may be found and fuller citations are provided, see Crawford Gribben, *John Owen and English Puritanism: Experiences of Defeat*, Oxford Studies in Historical Theology (Oxford: Oxford University Press, 2016).

distant, he surrounded himself with friends and rivals of the quality of John Milton and Lucy Hutchinson. Sustaining long-term literary feuds with fellow Puritans like Richard Baxter, he was able to cultivate supportive relationships with former political enemies, including the Earl of Oxford and perhaps even Charles II and James, Duke of York. And he developed the ideas from which his erstwhile student John Locke would fashion the classical liberalism that lies at the heart of modern democratic culture.

These achievements were significant, but they were achieved alongside Owen's day job. In the 1640s, while England was engaged in two civil wars, he worked as a parish minister in Essex and established himself as a preacher of national importance. In the 1650s, during the short-lived English republic, he undertook a series of senior administrative positions in the University of Oxford while serving on a government committee that was tasked with creating a new national church. In the early 1660s, while many of his friends were hung, drawn, and quartered as victims of the restored administration of Charles II, he worked hard to evade persecution and to build bridges with former enemies. And from the later 1660s until his death, as hostility toward religious dissenters began to dissipate, he settled down to look after small Independent congregations, while intervening in the theological disputes that, he feared, were undermining the health of the dissenting churches at a time when God's judgment was being poured out on the nation and the future of English Protestantism was imperiled.

As these achievements suggest, Owen must have been one of the most productive inhabitants of early modern England. He certainly considered how to make his work efficient. In his writing, he took shortcuts, recycled material between separately published titles, lifted primary sources from recently published anthologies of quotations, and employed a research assistant, Henry Stubbe, on at least one occasion.[2] But his approach to time management was resolutely theological. He encouraged Christians to think carefully about their use of time. He was confident that "God gives us enough time for all that he requires of us" and that believers should balance what has to be completed against the time available to complete it.[3] He recognized the danger of overwork as well as the danger of underachievement: "Many men . . . trifle away their time and their souls, sowing the wind of empty hopes."[4] Most Puritans, encouraged by preachers who feared their listeners were never doing enough, faced the opposite temptation. Owen promoted balance. He understood that not all work was good work and that an overbusy life could encroach on the privilege of walking with God. He advised those Christians who struggled with competing responsibilities that "it is more tolerable that our duties of holiness and regard to God should intrench on the duties of our callings and employments in this world" than vice versa.[5] For God never calls us to "take more upon us than we have time well to perform it in."[6] It was grace, rather than activity, that sustained the busyness of true spirituality: "You may take this measure with you in all your duties;—if they increase to a reverence of God, they are from grace; if they do not, they are from gifts, and no way sanctify the soul wherein they are."[7] Owen was extraordinary, but he called on his readers to be extraordinary too, for he was

2. For a discussion of Owen's secondhand quotations, see Richard Snoddy, "A Display of Learning? Citations and Shortcuts in John Owen's *A Display of Arminianisme* (1643)," *Westminster Theological Journal* (forthcoming); Jane Stevenson, "Introduction," in *The Works of Lucy Hutchinson*, ed. Elizabeth Clarke, David Norbrook, and Jane Stevenson, with textual introductions by Jonathan Gibson and editorial assistance from Mark Burden and Alice Eardley (Oxford: Oxford University Press, 2018), 2:298.

3. Owen, *Works*, 6:230.
4. Owen, *Works*, 2:187.
5. Owen, *Works*, 6:230.
6. Owen, *Works*, 6:230.
7. Owen, *Works*, 9:344.

sure that the God who "gives us enough time for all that he requires" would weave the providence that would enable his readers' spiritual lives.

Yet for all his success, Owen's life was marked by sustained tragedy. He endured long periods of ill health and in the mid-1650s was thought to be on his deathbed. He was bereaved of each of his ten children, from 1647 to 1682, and of his first wife, in 1677. His second marriage, to a wealthy widow who was a member of his small congregation, may not always have been happy. For over two decades, after 1660, he pursued his ministry on the margins of the law. Owen's life was characterized by his experience of defeat. It was, in many ways, the perfect context for his consideration of the spiritual life as a life sustained by grace.

Owen's Life

Owen was born sometime in 1616 to a family living in the tiny village of Stadhampton, in Oxfordshire. The family was not especially wealthy, and neither were they especially rigorous in their religious views, despite the fact that Owen's father was a clergyman of the established church. Late in life, Owen described his father as "a Nonconformist all his days, and a painful labourer in the vineyard of the Lord," but it is not clear that his father was committed to any program of reform within the English church in the 1610s and 1620s.[8] Owen's father was not among those Puritans whose dissatisfaction with the Church of England drove them into exile in the Netherlands or the New World, for he remained within the ecclesiastical establishment, apparently neglecting to fulfill some aspects of his liturgical duties, as was common among the party of conforming Puritans, whose hopes for further reformation had ended shortly after

---

8. Owen, *Works*, 13:224.

the accession of James I. Owen's description of his father may reflect the kindness of a dimmed memory, a filial piety that wanted to distinguish him from those elements of the liturgical practice of the established church that Owen, throughout his life, found most objectionable. Rather than being the heir of a radical tradition, therefore, Owen grew up in a religious community that had worked hard for the reformation of the Church of England and had failed. He remembered, as a boy, being told defamatory stories about "Brownists and Puritans," which he later found out to be false.[9] Owen grew up knowing the bitter reality of defeat.

Owen's sense of the marginal status of the religious community to which he belonged would have been confirmed during his university studies in the Queen's College, Oxford, which he commenced at the age of twelve, in 1628. This was not an especially young age at which to begin university education in the early seventeenth century—and in fact, the English universities were admitting a higher proportion of young men than in many other periods. But this expansion of university education came alongside the introduction of a number of controversial structural changes that made Owen's college days tumultuous. During the late 1620s and 1630s, the Queen's College, with the rest of the university, passed through a religious revolution, as the Reformed theological consensus that had dominated theological discussion for several decades was replaced by a new theological system, which seemed to its critics to mimic Catholic styles of worship and which questioned elemental components of English Protestant identity. Within Queen's, the debate provoked threats of violence, with one academic threatening to stab the provost, who was driving forward the controversial liturgical changes. The death threat was a sign of things

---

9. Owen, *Works*, 8:197.

to come, for England was shortly to enter a long civil war, in which religious ideas would be used to justify horrific levels of violence. Diaries from the period illustrate both the excitement of undergraduate life within the college and the growing pressures for teaching fellows to find ways to shoehorn their old religious principles into the new liturgical mold.

Some of the college community could not accommodate their consciences to the new rules. At the age of twenty-one, nine years after his admission to the Queen's College, Owen had graduated with his bachelor of arts and master of arts degrees and was likely a junior member of the teaching faculty. His hard study had earned him a place among the postgraduate students, and he may have been working toward his bachelor of divinity. But after years of preparation for an academic or clerical career, Owen felt that he had to leave Oxford. He could not support the religious innovations that were being pushed through Queen's with the support of the provost and through the university with the support of the vice-chancellor. The new and fashionable Arminianism ran entirely counter to a number of his convictions. Choosing conscience over career, Owen left the university in 1637.

It is not clear where or how Owen spent the next few years of his life. In the few surviving glimpses of his life during this period, Owen seems to have made erratic and unpredictable decisions. In 1638, within a year of abandoning his academic career, he sought ordination as a priest at the hands of the bishop of Oxford, one of the chief supporters of the Arminian innovations, at an age younger than that permitted by the canons.[10] He then found employment as a chaplain in the home of Sir Robert Dormer, a suspected Catholic whose riotous recreational

---

10. The details of Owen's ordination used in previous biographical accounts are here corrected by the information contained in the Clergy of the Church of England Database, https://theclergydatabase.org.uk, ref. 14413.

activities suggested no sympathy for Puritan views. By 1642, Owen had accepted another position as a household chaplain, this time in the home of Sir John Lovelace. Throughout this period, Owen appears to have been suffering from depression. It is possible that his move to the Lovelace household occurred around the same time that his father and elder brother took up new pastoral charges in the vicinity—though as a cause or consequence of Owen's movements, we cannot tell. As so often in accounts of Owen's life, we are left to balance possibilities. But it is possible that members of the family, which appears to have been close-knit, were deliberately regrouping to support their brother in his discouragement and, possibly, fear.

For fear was in the air. In the summer of 1642, England drifted into its First Civil War. That same summer, Owen officiated as household chaplain to a young married couple whose cousin, Richard Lovelace, would become one of the most eminent literary figures within the emerging party of royalists. Dormer and Lovelace, both of whom had employed Owen, declared in favor of the king. Owen, who did not need to express any political preference, decided in favor of Parliament. Having abandoned the university and his first employer, he now left the Lovelace household and the path into pastoral work it represented, and he traveled to London, without obvious prospects and almost entirely without friends. In the capital, one of the largest and most international cities in Europe, Owen found lodgings in Smithfield, a cheap and unpleasant place to live, close to the red-light district and to the place where one century before so many Protestant leaders had been martyred.

It was in this unpromising situation that Owen found his purpose in life. As censorship collapsed, Owen began to write, developing a manuscript on the priesthood of Christ that he never published. More important, he experienced a protracted crisis of assurance, an experience in which the "law seems sometimes to prevail, sin and Satan to rejoice; and the poor soul is filled with dread about its inheritance."[11] But this dejection was brought to a sudden end in an unexpected manner. Owen was sermon gadding, attending a church service along with his cousin in the hope of listening to preaching by a famous divine. But the famous preacher did not arrive. His replacement seemed to be much less promising, and Owen's cousin wanted to leave the service to seek better homiletical prospects elsewhere. But Owen, then in one of his periodic bouts of ill health, did not feel well enough to move. He stayed and found the unknown preacher directly addressing his spiritual situation. He never discovered the identity of this man. Under this unknown ministry, and on an unknown date, Owen was born again.

Owen's conversion came around the same time that he began his career as an author. For the first time, perhaps, he came to understand how the doctrines that had been so fiercely debated during the previous decade could bring peace to his troubled soul. And so, with new resolve, he threw himself into another writing project, *A Display of Arminianism*, which he dedicated to a committee of members of Parliament (MPs) that oversaw the religious health of the nation. It was not an auspicious first publication, for Owen was still learning how to construct an argument with clarity, accuracy, and discretion. It is not clear, as recent scholars have noted, that his depiction of his theological antagonists was entirely fair, and Owen certainly erred in including a prominent Presbyterian member of the Westminster Assembly among his targets.[12] Nevertheless, gaining the attention of his parliamentary patrons, Owen found the support he needed to enter parish ministry.

---

11. Owen, *Works*, 2:241.
12. Owen, *Works*, 10:22, 76.

The committee of MPs appointed Owen to his first parish, in Fordham, Essex. Finally settling into parish ministry, he became frustrated by the spiritual apathy of his parishioners. Within a few years, he had married a girl from the neighboring village of Coggeshall and had started a family. But in the later 1640s, as poor weather and a series of bad harvests resulted in widespread dearth, and as smallpox raged in the region, John and Mary buried several of their children. At Coggeshall, Owen was initially excited by the possibility of a new start, not least because the parish's previous minister had become a member of the Westminster Assembly. Large crowds came to hear him preach, with some suggestions that over two thousand people attended his sermons. But this was not a sign of an unusual spiritual awakening—his parishioners were legally compelled to attend worship. And within a few years, he was again disappointed by the spiritual condition of his parish and was again lamenting its disorder.

Owen's disappointment with the realities of parish ministry developed as he changed his views on church order. In his early parish ministry, he moved from supporting a rather unformed Presbyterianism to adopting the vision of church life that was then being promoted by Congregationalists. There may have been much less to this movement than some later historians have suggested, for in the period before the Westminster Confession of Faith (1647), the "Presbyterian" label was widely applied to those Puritans who pushed for further reform within the Church of England without supporting any detailed manifesto of the organizational changes that might entail. But Owen's growing sense of the need to emphasize the autonomy of individual congregations involved much more than defining his ecclesiological concerns.

Owen's neighbor, the Presbyterian minister Ralph Josselin, recorded in his diary the ways in which the Coggeshall church was changing. Owen installed an elder, John Sams, and had him preach without any ordination, even as he downplayed the importance of his own ordination. Sams was examined by the Westminster Assembly and supported for ordination several years after he began his ministry as a teaching elder in Owen's congregation. In addition, Owen gathered believers together for weeknight Bible study meetings, in which multiple people participated, in a move that might have been seen to undermine the special status of the congregation's teachers. And Owen also revised his views on the Lord's Supper, moving gradually to the position that the Eucharist should be celebrated weekly, by a gathered church rather than by members of a parish—and this while his neighbor Josselin abandoned the observance of the sacrament for a decade. These were notable departures from the norms of church life in the period—and in Owen's case, as so often in Christian history thereafter, key indicators of an impulse to recover as accurately as possible the order of the New Testament churches. For Owen was also revising his views of baptism, moving steadily away from the very high view of the efficacy of baptism that he outlined in his first publication to adopt in the 1650s a perspective on the sacrament that made sense of his growing sympathy for and cooperation with Baptists.

Owen's new vision of church life developed in startling contrast to the clerical, formal, and liturgical preferences of his Presbyterian colleagues. The Blasphemy Act of 1648, which was supported by Presbyterian MPs and which sought to provide legal safeguards for the achievements of the Westminster Assembly, criminalized adherence to a range of religious opinions, making any defense of believers baptism, for example, a penal offense. The most effective opposition to this Presbyterian theocracy was located in the army, and Owen increasingly identified himself with the leaders of its opposition to the civilian government that seemed increasingly unlikely to support the kind of reformation of church and state that he had envisaged. In 1648, he witnessed the siege of Colchester, a large town five miles from Coggeshall. It was Owen's first direct experience of the Civil Wars, and it must have been harrowing. Some of the worst war crimes of the period were committed during that long summer siege. But if Owen was disturbed by the crimes against civilians and the horrific mutilation of animals, he did not refer to it in the sermons he preached celebrating the achievements of the parliamentary soldiers and their general, Sir Thomas Fairfax. These sermons brought him to the attention of the army leaders whom he had come to admire. As the political mood darkened and, in the winter of 1648–1649, the king was put on trial and executed, Owen's new patrons within the high military command identified him as the man to commemorate the English Revolution.

For the revolution made Owen. One day after the execution of Charles I, who had been convicted of treason, Owen addressed MPs with an oration that understood, without celebrating, the achievements of regicide. He, like his patrons, had something to gain from the new situation of England. Owen's links with the army pulled him further from parish ministry and brought him into contact with Oliver Cromwell. Owen's relationship with this extraordinary and brilliant military leader was initially very close. He accompanied Cromwell on the invasion of Ireland in 1649, remaining in Dublin, where for the first time he believed his ministry was being attended with conversions. His journey to Scotland in 1650 was more complicated, for he was drawn into the complex politics and internal divisions of the kirk. But the English forces themselves may have begun to fracture: Archibald Johnston of Wariston, the

Scottish Covenanter leader, heard Owen preach in Berwick a sermon that he understood as attacking Cromwell's pride.[13] In spring 1651, Owen left the army, looking for new opportunities, and was awarded with positions of academic leadership in the university from which he had resigned less than fifteen years earlier.

Owen's return to Oxford in summer 1651 was a moment of triumph. As dean of Christ Church, and later vice-chancellor of the university, Owen was given the opportunity to reshape the institution, to protect Reformed theology, and to promote godliness among the staff and students. He pursued these ends with diligence, generosity, and occasionally with a lack of scruple. It was a difficult and demanding career transition. The move to Oxford had pushed him away from the moral clarity of civil war and into the ambiguous and complex world of academic politics. There is some evidence that he struggled to know how best to negotiate his new environment. Though all these appointments represented the apex of his career, they also represented some of his greatest challenges.

Owen preached and wrote relentlessly throughout his years in Oxford. A number of the books he completed during the 1650s have become spiritual classics, including his devotional handbooks *Of the Mortification of Sin in Believers* (1656) and *Of Communion with God* (1658). But as his Scottish sermons had earlier suggested, he was also becoming increasingly critical of the government. It was obvious that the army, not Parliament, held the real political power, even as Cromwell's court grew increasingly similar to that of the king it had replaced. Owen grew worried and tried to intervene in a complex political situation. Then, uncharacteristically, he overreached himself. In 1654, he

---

13. *Diary of Sir Archibald Johnston of Wariston* (Edinburgh: Scottish History Society, 1911), 2:16.

was elected as an MP for the first Protectoral Parliament. In the few months that he spent in the Commons, he was associated with radical republicans, men who were alarmed by the increasingly monarchical trappings of the Cromwell family. Critical observers noted that Owen was among a group of MPs who were of "a contrary judgement to Cromwell."[14] Within months, Owen was expelled from Parliament on the basis that he was a clergyman and therefore ineligible to sit in the house. But Owen denied the charge: he had rejected his ordination and the ontological difference between clergy and laity that it presupposed.

Back in Oxford, perhaps stinging from this defeat, Owen became ever more critical of the direction being taken by the government. He condemned the frivolity of Cromwell's court and intervened on behalf of army republicans to stop Cromwell being crowned king. By 1657, the breach with his old patron and friend was complete. Owen did not see Cromwell as he gradually sickened and, in September 1658, died. When Oliver was replaced by Richard, his son, who wished to continue the conservative trend of his father's administration, Owen moved to gather a congregation of disaffected republicans among the military leadership. The church gathered in Wallingford House, and Philip Nye preached at its constitution, giving Owen a pastoral charge that exhorted him to fulfill the duties of an elder.[15] But this congregation appears to have thrown its efforts into political activities. In a complex series of events, its members worked to undermine the new government before it had any opportunity to consolidate its power. The army had brought down governments before. In fact, several Parliaments since the regicide had been ended by the army's intervention. But this time, the officers who met at Wallingford House gambled and lost.

---

14. *Diary of Sir Archibald Johnston of Wariston*, 2:287.
15. Notebook of Smith Fleetwood, MS Comm. 1, pp. 24–36, University of Edinburgh, New College.

Their coup created chaos until Charles II returned. Owen's criticisms of the Cromwellian government had helped undermine it.

The Restoration of the monarchy in May 1660 ended the English Revolution. Its leaders were tried, found guilty of treason, and publicly butchered. Meanwhile, the ejection of Puritan ministers from the Church of England in August 1662 ended any hope that the godly could be accommodated within the established church. Owen, who was in some personal danger, struggled to know how best to respond to the new circumstances. His activities in the early 1660s reveal his mental conflict. In January 1661, while he was leading a conventicle, his house was raided by the local militia, who carried away a half dozen cases of pistols. Throughout the same period, his books advocated a surprising and not entirely consistent range of positions. In *Animadversions on a Treatise Intituled Fiat Lux* (1662) and its *Vindication* (1664), for example, Owen praised the new king as the greatest Protestant in Europe, defended his role as the head of the established church, spoke highly of the Church of England's Thirty-Nine Articles, and denied the need for imposing confessions of faith. In other publications from this period, he defended Independent church order and called for congregations to strenuously defend confessional Reformed theology. All these works were published anonymously, and some of them were published illegally. Owen was wise to exercise caution. The impaled heads of several of his old friends were still on display in London. There was every chance that he, too, could become a victim of the restored regime.

But the political situation began to settle. By the mid-1660s, after the devastating outbreak of the Great Plague (1665–1666) and the Great Fire (1666), nonconformists gained the courage to return to public preaching, even in London. Owen kept his head down, continued writing, and found time in 1668 to pose for a portrait by one of the most fashionable of the court painters. By the early 1670s, his situation had changed again. His small congregation, which comprised around thirty individuals, many of them prominent republicans with close links to the party that had undermined the English Revolution, merged with a congregation of around one hundred individuals, which had been led by the recently deceased Puritan preacher Joseph Caryl. They began to meet on the premises that belonged to the larger congregation on Leadenhall Street, London.

Owen's preaching changed to address the new situation. With a more diverse congregation, his sermons were shorter, more focused, and geared very directly to the pastoral needs of his listeners. In many ways, these sermons represent some of the best of his work. He moved away from the extended topical and exegetical series that had featured in his earlier ministry to instead present different themes and passages each week. Perhaps many members of his new congregation had grown tired of the preaching of extended series of sermons—after all, Caryl's exposition of Job had lasted for more than two decades. Owen's new method of preaching drew crowds, and perhaps for the first time, he became a genuinely popular preacher.

We get our clearest view of Owen's pastoral concerns in the materials that survive from this period of his ministry. He found it a terribly difficult time. Now in his early sixties, Owen was surrounded by death. Mary, his wife, died in 1677, and their last surviving child died in 1682. Despite his second marriage, his friends remarked on his continuing depression. He had lost so much—a wife, each of his children, and, he worried, the work of a lifetime. Owen looked across the spectrum of English dissent and persuaded himself that the churches were in ruins. When he died, in August 1683, Owen believed that the Puritan project had failed and that, with the openly Catholic James,

Duke of York, almost certain to succeed his brother as king, the English Reformation was almost over.

Of course, events proved otherwise. The reign of James II generated its own instabilities, creating the panic throughout the political nation that led to his forced abdication and to MPs inviting the invasion of William of Orange (1688). The Glorious Revolution that followed secured the British Protestant constitution, but it did not secure the integrity of the dissenting churches. After his death, Owen's congregation did not long continue in his theological footsteps. Isaac Watts, his successor in the pastoral office, experimented with Trinitarian doctrine to such an extent that, by the 1720s, London Unitarians were suggesting that he had come to support their cause.

But some evangelicals did continue to appreciate Owen's legacy. Surprisingly, perhaps, it was John Wesley who kept Owen's reputation alive when he republished parts of Owen's writing in his *Christian Library* (1750). Throughout the eighteenth century, Scottish publishers kept his ecclesiastical works in print, while a much smaller number of English publishers reprinted his devotional and exegetical works. In the nineteenth century, Owen was praised by the Exclusive Brethren leader William Kelly, even as he was abominated by liberal evangelicals within the Church of Scotland. In the early twentieth century, he found appreciative readers in A. W. Pink in the 1920s and D. Martyn Lloyd-Jones in the 1930s, both of whom would spearhead the revival of British Calvinism, and also in Jim Eliot, the future missionary martyr, in the early 1950s. And so, when the Banner of Truth republished *The Death of Death in the Death of Christ* (1959), as a prelude to their republication of William Goold's edition of Owen's *Works* (1965–1968), the stage was already set for Owen's recovery. Sixty years later, Owen may have more readers than he ever had before.

Reading Owen

This book is an introduction to Owen's life and thought. It builds on the growing number of studies of his theological work, many of which reflect the concern of Richard A. Muller, and others, to take seriously the intellectual claims of the writers of post-Reformation Reformed dogmatics.[16] Many of these books offer detailed and formidable reconstructions of Owen's formulation of key doctrines. They have considered Owen as a high Calvinist theologian, presenting detailed accounts of his doctrine of God, Christology, soteriology, ecclesiology, and eschatology.[17] A much smaller body of work has considered his role as preacher to the Long Parliament, as chaplain to the Cromwellian invasions of Ireland and Scotland, as dean of Christ Church, Oxford, as vice-chancellor of the University of Oxford, as architect of the Cromwellian religious settlement, as defender of the toleration of dissenters after the Restoration, and as a widely published author of theological polemic, biblical commentary, and political intervention.[18] This book also draws on work by those authors who have offered new light on

16. Owen is a significant figure in the tradition represented in Richard A. Muller, *Post-Reformation Reformed Dogmatics: The Rise and Development of Reformed Orthodoxy, ca. 1520 to ca. 1725*, 4 vols. (Grand Rapids, MI: Baker Academic, 2003).

17. See, for example, Sinclair B. Ferguson, *John Owen on the Christian Life* (Edinburgh: Banner of Truth, 1987); Steve Griffiths, *Redeem the Time: Sin in the Writings of John Owen* (Fearn, Ross-shire, Scotland: Mentor, 2001); Richard W. Daniels, *The Christology of John Owen* (Grand Rapids, MI: Reformed Heritage Books, 2004); Brian K. Kay, *Trinitarian Spirituality: John Owen and the Doctrine of God in Western Devotion*, Studies in Christian History and Thought (Milton Keynes, UK: Paternoster, 2007); Alan Spence, *Incarnation and Inspiration: John Owen and the Coherence of Christology*, T&T Clark Theology (London: T&T Clark, 2007); Lee Gatiss, *From Life's First Cry: John Owen on Infant Baptism and Infant Salvation*, St. Antholin's Lectureship Charity Lecture 2008 (London: Latimer Trust, 2008); Kelly M. Kapic and Mark Jones, eds., *The Ashgate Research Companion to John Owen's Theology* (Aldershot, UK: Ashgate, 2012); Christopher Cleveland, *Thomism in John Owen* (Farnham, UK: Ashgate, 2013).

18. See, for example, Crawford Gribben, "Polemic and Apocalyptic in the Cromwellian Invasion of Scotland," *Literature & History* 23, no. 1 (2014): 1–18; Crawford Gribben, "John Owen, Renaissance Man? The Evidence of Edward Millington's *Bibliotheca Oweniana* (1684)," *Westminster Theological Journal* 72, no. 2 (2010): 321–32, reprinted in Kapic and Jones, *Ashgate Research Companion*, 97–109.

Owen's life and work by situating their reconstructions of his ideas within the relevant social, cultural, religious, and institutional contexts. Tim Cooper's masterful account *John Owen, Richard Baxter and the Formation of Nonconformity* (2011) set a new standard for a work in this field, describing the most important relationship—or rivalry—in seventeenth-century dissenting culture. In *John Owen and English Puritanism: Experiences of Defeat* (2016), I tried to extend this approach in a more narrowly focused theological biography. More recently, Martyn Cowan's excellent work *John Owen and the Civil War Apocalypse: Preaching, Prophecy and Politics* (2018) has shown how this contextual approach can open up entirely new research questions and can challenge some widely shared assumptions about Owen's convictions and achievements. This contextual approach is still quite new, and most work on Owen continues to focus on the reconstruction of his doctrine, but there are signs of increasing interest in a more rounded appreciation of his life.

These different kinds of works on Owen are mutually enriching and are being developed as audiences for Owen's work are growing and diversifying. Owen is finding increasing numbers of readers within the church. In the last decade, several of his most important titles have been rendered into modern English, and Crossway is undertaking to publish his complete works in modernized language. At the same time, within the academy, books about Owen are being advertised less often by religious publishers and more often by their academic peers. This is an exciting signal that scholars outside the Reformed tradition are paying more attention to one of the most significant English Protestant thinkers. Some purists may not be pleased that Owen is being adapted for new markets. The popularizing and contextual tendencies will always be controversial, but fortunately, those who promote these various new approaches have less cause than their subject to complain of reviewers who "only filched out of the whole what he thought he could wrest unto his end, and scoffingly descant upon."[19] Whatever their approach, Owen's readers have yet to exhaust the significance of his eight million words.

Within these contexts, this book is attempting to do something new. It offers an introduction to Owen's work but one that is framed around his representation of the spiritual life. Owen was notoriously reluctant to share details of his own life experiences but wrote at great length about his expectations of the lives of others. For Owen, the introduction to spiritual life began in childhood, with baptism and instruction in the faith. He expected that baptized and catechized children would in due course make the profession of faith that would permit them to become members of a local church. Church membership was not a rite of passage but a status conferred only on those who could narrate an experience of conversion, which claim had to be supported by a serious and purposeful lifestyle. In his preaching to young people, Owen presented his high Calvinist theology in sometimes astonishing ways, attempting to inspire his listeners with the almost mystical delights of knowing God in three persons. This style of presentation was made possible by his scholastic theology, but it certainly did not emphasize scholastic method. Owen's depiction of the challenges of maturity and adulthood recognized the complexity of life at home, in the church, and in society. His contributions to Restoration political theory and to the Scientific Revolution that presaged the Enlightenment show him to be seriously engaged with the cultural challenges affecting Protestant nonconformists. And especially as he grew older, Owen thought a great deal about

---

19. Owen, *Works*, 2:314.

death. While he lost seven of his ten children during the 1640s and 1650s, his discussion of death, the intermediate state, resurrection, and final glory intensified after the spectacularly horrific executions of those of his friends and colleagues who had high profiles during the Civil Wars and republic and, especially in the 1670s and early 1680s, with the deaths of his first wife, his congregants, his colleagues in ministry, and his last surviving daughter.

Owen's description of spiritual life was developed through one of the most tumultuous centuries in English history. He lived through three monarchies, a civil war, and a republic, and he participated in two invasions. He had to respond as a pastor to the collapse of the Cromwellian regime, the Fire of London, and the Great Plague. And after celebrating the achievements of the republic, as one of its most high-profile religious leaders, he had to work out how Christians should respond to the experience of political defeat and the providential significance of powerlessness, when everything he had worked for had melted into air.

But Owen understood what death meant—and in whom death found meaning. Christians could find death "light" when they remembered "who is the stay of their lives and the end of their death."[20] For Owen, like Paul, to live was Christ and to die was gain (Phil. 1:21). In its continuation and its end, spiritual life was centered on Jesus Christ. Always modest in self-references, Owen regarded himself as having "the least experience" of communion with Christ "of all the saints of God," but he claimed to have found in that communion "that in it which is better than ten thousand worlds" and sought to spend (speaking of himself in the third person) "the residue of the few and evil days of his pilgrimage in pursuit hereof,—in the con-

---

20. Owen, *Works*, 2:137.

templations of the excellencies, desirableness, love, and grace of our dear Lord Jesus."[21] For Owen understood that the "few and evil days of pilgrimage," when passed in fellowship with Christ, transformed the "wretched world" in an experience of grace, from birth to death, and far beyond, in a continually deepening spiritual life.[22]

21. Owen, *Works*, 2:154.
22. Owen, *Works*, 2:154.

1

Childhood

John Owen's account of the life of grace began at birth. Owen
was an able and sensitive theologian of childhood—and one of
the earliest of English children's authors. After several years of
parish ministry in Essex during the years of bad harvests and
dearth of the later 1640s and the deaths of three of his children
under the age of five, Owen became acutely aware of the brevity
of childhood and the responsibility of parents and churches to
prepare their young people for the present life as well as the life
to come. In his published writings and extant sermons, Owen
maintained that the children of believers should be baptized and
that their Christian formation began with this baptism, but his
rationale for this practice and his beliefs about its effect changed
considerably over the course of his career, especially in the early
1650s, when he began to work alongside Baptists and accepted
that his new friends' understanding of the sacrament and Christian initiation did not represent fundamental theological error.

As his convictions about baptismal practice moderated, and
after the deaths of several more of his children in the 1650s,

Owen remained convinced that the children of believers ought to be instructed in the faith and that the child's family and congregation should work together to achieve this end. He addressed this responsibility in two catechisms that he published in 1645, during the period of his parish ministry, and in *The Primer*, which he published in 1652, after taking up his role as a university administrator at Oxford. His catechisms are well known, were reprinted within his lifetime, and follow the familiar model of matching questions and answers to provide instruction on core themes in Christian doctrine. But Owen's *Primer* is much less well known. It is not included in the best-known edition of his work, a set of twenty-four volumes that appeared in the mid-nineteenth century and has (mostly) been kept in print by Banner of Truth, and it has slipped out of sight of the many historians and theologians who continue to study Owen's work. Yet *The Primer* deserves to be recovered. It reveals how this formidable Puritan theologian imagined the ideal Christian home—and illustrates the simplicity and warmth that he thought appropriate for the nurture of Christian children.

It is not clear how Owen's depiction of family life compared to his own experience, either as a parent or a child. He wrote very little about his own childhood, in Stadhampton, Oxfordshire, in the late 1610s and 1620s. He remembered his father, a clergyman within the Church of England, apparently with affection, and he maintained in later life close connections with his brothers and sisters. Stadhampton represented a fixed point in Owen's turning world. When his public career ended with the collapse of the republic, in the early 1660s he returned to live in the village, where his sister was married to the minister of the parish church and was raising the third generation of the family to live in the vicinity. His own experience of fatherhood was marked by deaths and disappointments and was something that, one early admirer admitted, he had not "much injoyed."[1]

But the fact that Owen retained his connection with Stadhampton throughout his long life is not to suggest that he had always found the community to be sympathetic to his beliefs. As a schoolboy, Owen recognized that the faith that was encouraged in the family home was ridiculed in the world, hearing "a hundred times" stories about "Brownists and Puritans" that slandered the godly but that, he later discovered, were "forgeries of Pagans . . . imposed on the primitive Christians."[2] In response to this criticism, the family home may have sustained a narrative culture of its own. "When a child is abused abroad in the streets by strangers," Owen recalled, "he runs with speed to the bosom of his father . . . and is comforted."[3] Owen later remembered examples of the "pretty midnight story" that would be "told to bring children asleep."[4] The opposition and criticism of the world may have been met in the minister's house in Stadhampton by the warmth and kindness of bedtime routines.

It is also unclear how Owen's depiction of family life compared to his experience as a parent. Owen married Mary Rooke in 1643. It would have been a day of extraordinary happiness for the young preacher. Wedding days were occasions of great joy for happy couples, he suggested, "the day of the gladness of their hearts," later remembering that the "delight of the bridegroom in the day of his espousals is the height of what an expression of delight can be carried unto."[5] John and Mary soon became parents. And contrary to the expectations of those historians who imagine that high rates of child mortality in early

1. *A Vindication of the Late Reverend and Learned John Owen D.D.* (London, 1684), 37–38.
2. Owen, *Works*, 8:177, 197.
3. Owen, *Works*, 2:38.
4. Owen, *Works*, 14:153.
5. Owen, *Works*, 2:54, 118.

modernity must have encouraged emotionally distant parenting, Owen may have been an indulgent father. He remembered "how unwilling is a child to come into the presence of an angry father" and thought that if the "correction of a son argues a great provocation," the correction of an only son must be caused by the "greatest [provocation] imaginable."[6] He may well have followed his own advice in building emotional connections between parents and children: "If the love of a father will not make a child delight in him, what will?"[7]

But John and Mary Owen soon experienced tragedy. Their oldest children were born during one of the worst periods of dearth in English history. Owen's friend, neighbor, and clerical colleague Ralph Josselin recorded in his diary some extraordinary accounts of the cold summers and wet winters in the later 1640s that left cattle starving in the fields and children dying of disease. Owen referred to the excessive rain and short harvests of these years in a sermon in January 1649.[8] The environmental tragedy was touching his own home too: the firstborn, John, who was born in 1644, witnessed the deaths of his sisters, Mary and Elizah (d. 1647), and brother, Thomas (d. 1648), before his own death in 1649. Owen never described the impact of these deaths on Mary or the pain and terrible emptiness of their suddenly childless home.

Nevertheless, it was during this difficult period that Owen's thoughts turned to the instruction of children and to their formation in Christian faith. Owen's thoughts about child-rearing were often quite practical—as when, for example, he warned against giving children too much money.[9] But his principal concern was for the spiritual welfare of children in Christian homes. He recognized that the warm affection that he encour-

---

6. Owen, *Works*, 2:35, 96.
7. Owen, *Works*, 2:36.
8. Owen, *Works*, 8:151.
9. Owen, *Works*, 8:81.

aged in Christian families could never ensure the salvation of their children: "We cannot love grace into a child. . . . We cannot love them into heaven, though it may be the great desire of our soul. It was love that made Abraham cry, 'O that Ishmael might live before thee!' but it might not be."[10] And so Owen's earliest writing illustrated the importance he placed on the baptism and spiritual nurture of the children of Christian parents. His catechisms provided a simple, precise, and well-rounded introduction to Christian teaching. While these publications were addressed to adults, a short pamphlet that he published provided its intended audience of "young learners" with basic skills in literacy and numeracy while teaching the elements of Reformed Christianity and encouraging family routines that emphasized gratitude and prayer.

This chapter considers Owen's account of Christian childhood, from the intitiation represented in baptism, through its formation within the home, to its preparation for full communion with the church by means of catechism. For Owen, the grace that sustained spiritual life began in a distinctively Christian childhood.

Baptism

Like other Reformed theologians, Owen thought a great deal about the sacraments. In the early decades of the Reformation, Reformed theologians came to agree that the true church could be distinguished from the false church by its proper administration of baptism and the Lord's Supper. This claim, which recognized the proper administration of the sacraments as one of the three "marks" of the church, reflected the Protestant emphasis on the simplification of sacramental theology, by means of which the seven sacraments of the Catholic Church were

---

10. Owen, *Works*, 2:63.

reduced in their number and, in many but not all cases, their effect. Debates about the sacraments defined the parties that were contesting the direction of Protestant reform. Reformed theologians had to articulate their theology of baptism against the claims of Catholics on one side and Anabaptists on the other. Their struggle was to maintain a biblical middle way. After all, they considered, if Catholics claimed too much for the power of baptism, Anabaptists reduced it to being no more than a sign. If Catholics wished to provide baptism to every child born under their jurisdiction, Anabaptists wished to restrict it to those who could believe. If Catholics aligned baptism with entry into the body politic, Anabaptists limited it to entry into the church. Owen developed his theology of baptism in reaction to these competing claims but also in response to the changing political circumstances of the mid-seventeenth century, the rise and fall of the Presbyterian party during the English Civil Wars, and his ongoing reading of Scripture. He thought it possible that children could be born again "before they come to the use of reason, or in their infancy."[11] But he did not link baptism to this experience of saving grace. His rationale for the practice of infant baptism certainly evolved, but Owen consistently argued that it marked the child's entry into the care of the local congregation, if not into its actual membership, and that baptism in that sense marked the beginning of Christian nurture.

Owen "wrote little about baptism," although he thought about the sacrament throughout his career.[12] He inherited a high view of baptism from the English Reformers. In his earliest reference to baptism, in a book published in 1643, Owen argued that baptism does something: it takes away "that which hinders

11. Owen, *Works*, 3:213.
12. Ryan M. McGraw, *A Heavenly Directory: Trinitarian Piety, Public Worship and a Reassessment of John Owen's Theology* (Bristol, CT: Vandenhoeck & Ruprecht, 2014), 111.

our salvation; which is not the first sin of Adam imputed, but our own inherent lust and pollution."[13] This was an unusual position for a Puritan minister to adopt, echoing as it did the *ex opere operato* model of the medieval and Catholic church, in which the benefits of baptism were automatically conferred on the infant in the administration of the rite—although Catholic theologians taught that baptism removed the stain of original sin, rather than actual transgressions. But Owen was not alone in making these kinds of claims. One of the most important members of the Westminster Assembly, Cornelius Burgess, had made similar arguments in a book published in Oxford around the same time that Owen began his undergraduate studies in that city.[14] For Burgess, the idea that baptism was in some way related to the regeneration of elect infants was well within the orthodox boundaries of English Reformed thought. It seems likely that Owen shared a version of this position in arguing that baptism removes "our own inherent lust and pollution." But he quickly revised this claim.

Owen began to moderate his high view of the efficacy of baptism. In his first catechism, in 1645, he moved away from this argument about inherent sin to argue instead that baptism effected the adoption of the baptized child, by bringing the child into God's family. Baptism, he instructed his parishioners, is "an holy Ordinance, whereby being sprinkled with water according to Christ's institution, we are by his grace made children of God, and have the promises of the Covenant sealed unto us."[15] Owen's later writing did not enlarge on this idea, perhaps because the Westminster Assembly, then meeting to define the

---

13. Owen, *Works*, 10:80.

14. Cornelius Burgess, *Baptismall Regeneration of Elect Infants Professed by the Church of England, according to the Scriptures, the Primitive Church, the Present Reformed Churches, and Many Particular Divines Apart* (Oxford, 1629); cf. Thomas Crosfield, *The Diary of Thomas Crosfield*, ed. F. S. Boas (London: Oxford University Press, 1935), 38.

15. Owen, *Works*, 1:469.

orthodoxy of the established churches of England, was coming to a different conclusion, arguing against the view that baptism achieved something by insisting that baptisms should be carried out because of a preexisting reality. The liturgical handbook that the Westminster Assembly published argued that the children of believers should be baptized because they were already "Christians, and federally holy before Baptisme," and not, as Owen had insisted, made children of God by that sacramental action.[16] This was a slight but significant revision.

Owen continued to think through the doctrine, learning from the Westminster Assembly's Confession, if not its Directory for Public Worship, as he did so. By 1652, he had adopted the position that he would maintain for the rest of his writing career, defining baptism as "an holy institution of Jesus Christ, wherein the washing with water in the name of the Father, and of the Son, and of the Holy Ghost, is a sign and seal of my washing with the Blood and Spirit of Christ, of my ingrafting into him, and pardon of sin thereby."[17] Adding the Trinitarian formula, and drawing on the Augustinian language of sign and seal, Owen had arrived at a definition of baptism that was solidly biblical and would become widely accepted, even among those who differed from Owen on the question of its proper subjects.

And so, in the early 1650s, as the Westminster divines completed the work of the assembly, Owen continued to moderate the high view of baptism that his earliest publications had assumed. Perhaps significantly, this move seems to have occurred as he began to spend a significant amount of time working alongside other Puritans who argued that baptism should be restricted to those who could make a credible profession of faith. From 1652, Owen worked with prominent Baptists on a

---

16. [Westminster Assembly,] *A Directory for the Publique Worship of God throughout the Three Kingdomes* (London, 1645), 20.

17. John Owen, *The Primer* (London, 1652), n.p.

series of high-profile committees that were tasked with guiding the religious policy of the new republic, overseeing the accuracy of printed Bibles, managing a project for a new translation of Scripture (which never materialized), and monitoring appointments to the list of preachers whose salaries were provided by the state. Owen's expectations of the effects of baptism moderated as this work continued. In 1652, as we have just noticed, he abandoned his earlier speculations about the achievements of baptism to emphasize instead its significance as sign and seal. In 1654, he was arguing against the doctrine of baptismal regeneration.[18] In 1656, he described baptism as assisting in sanctification by acting as a visible reminder of the believer's status: "We have in baptism an evidence of our implantation into Christ; we are baptized into him" in "his death." Our being "baptized into the death of Christ" represents the mortification of our corruptions, with our total "conformity" to the experience of Christ, "so that as he was raised up to glory, we may be raised up to grace and newness of life."[19]

These arguments confirmed his position that baptism was a sign and seal, but he was also willing to tolerate others with different beliefs. Through much of the 1650s, he sat on committees that were tasked with constructing a statement of faith to establish the boundaries of belief for the Cromwellian national church. The most detailed document that this committee prepared, "A New Confession of Faith," which was privately circulated in 1654, made no mention at all of the sacraments. By the mid-1650s, as his own views on sacramental efficacy were moderating, Owen had conceded that the denial of infant baptism did not represent fundamental theological error.

---

18. Owen, *Works*, 11:552.
19. Owen, *Works*, 6:84.

Owen could downplay the significance of the rejection of infant baptism because he was rethinking the role of baptism in the Christian life. He came to distinguish baptism not just from the application of salvation but also from the experience of joining a church. In 1657, he argued that baptism "precedes admission into church membership, as to a particular church; the subjects of it . . . have right unto it, whether they be joined to any particular church or no" (his insistence that "this judgment hath been my constant and uninterrupted practice," like his other claims to consistency, should not be taken at face value).[20] And as he extrapolated the sacrament from its traditional role as providing entrance to church membership, he also concluded that those who rejected the doctrine of infant baptism and who subjected themselves to what might be considered a second baptism should not be considered schismatic. Of course, there were some very unfortunate historical precedents for the practice of rebaptism, he recognized, but seventeenth-century Baptists were not Donatists. Baptists "do the same thing" as Donatists, he recognized, "but not on the same principles." He understood the logic of his Baptist colleagues to be that infant baptism is "null from the nature of the thing itself, not the way of its administration," and so concluded that his Baptist friends, unlike the Donatists, were not claiming that they were the only true church, a claim that would properly have been considered schismatic.[21]

Owen's thinking through the doctrine of baptism and his conclusion that it provided neither salvation nor the status of church membership worked to the advantage of his new colleagues, who, he recognized, were denying their children an ordinance that, whatever its symbolic value, had no intrinsic

---

20. Owen, *Works*, 13:259.
21. Owen, *Works*, 13:184.

effect. Owen's about-face on baptism was lowering the stakes in one of the most significant theological debates of the seventeenth century. Recognizing that he had more in common with Baptists than with the Presbyterians with whom he had once been aligned, Owen enabled the theological détente that was being sustained in the cooperative efforts that underlay the search for a Cromwellian religious settlement.

For all this moderating of his views, however, Owen was still active among the Congregational churches. In autumn 1658, just weeks after the death of Oliver Cromwell, Owen met with other Congregational leaders to prepare a revision of the Westminster Confession that they could own as a statement of denominational faith. The Savoy Declaration, which they produced, restated the baptismal formulae of the Westminster divines; it did not allow the flexibility for baptism that Owen's more recent writing had explored, but it did confirm his emphasis on baptism as sign and seal.

After 1660, as the changing political circumstances of the Restoration of the monarchy initiated a brutal persecution, pushing dissenters together as a suffering community, Owen's thoughts turned again to the question of what baptism meant. In 1662, he recognized that the baptismal texts he had formerly read in realist terms should be understood metaphorically. He remembered that the early church required candidates to prepare for baptism through a scrupulous program of catechesis.[22] As a consequence, the apostles and the fathers who succeeded them regarded "all baptized, initiated persons, ingrafted into the church, as sanctified persons."[23] Owen made this claim while also defending the proposition, in *A Brief Instruction in the Worship of God* (1667), that the

---

22. Owen, *Works*, 15:23.
23. Owen, *Works*, 10:367.

"proper subjects of baptism" are "professing believers . . . and their infant seed," who, he reminded his readers, were not made members of the church by baptism.[24] The children of believers may not be church members, he recognized, but they were already "holy" (1 Cor. 7:14).

It was during this period that Owen published one of his longest and most considered discussions of baptism. In his exposition of Psalm 130 (1668), he emphasized that baptism was a sign, which represents the "certainty and truth of [God's] grace in pardon unto their senses by a visible pledge. [God] lets them know that he would take away their sin, wherein their spiritual defilement doth consist, even as water takes away the outward filth of the body."[25] Critically, Owen refused to "dispute . . . who are the proper immediate objects of [baptism]; whether they only who actually can make profession of their faith, or believers with their infant seed. For my part," he continued, "I believe that all whom Christ loves and pardons are to be made partakers of the pledge thereof."[26]

This was a very ambiguous defense of infant baptism, but it emphasized Owen's conviction that baptism stopped short of introducing its subject into church membership. For that to happen, Owen considered, in a posthumous publication, baptism should be followed by a period of appropriate spiritual nurture, "until they come unto such seasons wherein the personal performance of those duties whereon the continuation of the estate of visible regeneration doth depend is required of them."[27] At some point following childhood, those who had been baptized and instructed in the faith were to profess that faith and in so doing join the membership of a congregation.

---

24. Owen, *Works*, 15:512.
25. Owen, *Works*, 6:465–66.
26. Owen, *Works*, 6:466.
27. Owen, *Works*, 16:12.

Of course, he argued, some children of Christian families would not choose to do so: "Herein if they fail, they lose all privilege and benefit by their baptism."[28] For the blessings of baptism were conditional and time bound. Baptism was a sign of the "holy" status of the children of believers and could act as a "seal" of the faith that they professed. But for those who never professed faith, their baptism meant nothing.

Throughout his mature writing, Owen emphasized the blessings that were signaled but not achieved by baptism. Although he employed several theologies of baptism to support a single baptismal practice, he consistently regarded baptism as the beginning of Christian formation. Along with the preaching of the gospel, it was a means by which children born into Christian families would own their status as Christian disciples.[29] While baptism did not effect regeneration or inclusion within the church, and while, as a consequence, those who did not baptize their children were not guilty of schism or fundamental theological error, Owen still insisted that baptism was the "beginning and foundation of . . . all the other spiritual privileges."[30] It was the sign and seal of a distinctively Christian childhood—and signified the beginning of spiritual life.

Formation

Whatever his changing views on baptism and its effects, Owen understood that a child born into a Christian family had to be instructed in faith. In 1652, while undertaking senior administrative roles at the University of Oxford, Owen published *The Primer*, a small pamphlet, like others of a similar name, that sought to provide a basic educational resource for Christian children. This short work was designed to teach "young

---

28. Owen, *Works*, 16:12.
29. Owen, *Works*, 15:144.
30. Owen, *Works*, 7:18.

learners" how to read and how to recognize roman and arabic numbers, while also providing texts for memorization, including several psalms, chapters from the Gospels, the Lord's Prayer, the Apostles' Creed, and a basic catechism, which was focused on God's actions in creating the cosmos, in giving the law in the Ten Commandments, and in providing those who could not keep that law with a way of salvation. *The Primer* included prayers that were to be used before and after eating, as well as a morning prayer and two prayers for the evening (these prayers are reprinted in the appendix of this book).

The Primer is an extraordinary document. It affords a glimpse into the ideal Christian household as Owen imagined it. This ideal family would spend considerable time educating their children, but it would also structure its daily routine around worship. Its members would pray individually in the morning and evening, as well as before and after every meal. Owen did not expect these prayers to be long. Family members would be well instructed in the faith, and parents would be able to teach their children. These children would memorize entire chapters of Scripture and be able to draw on the riches of Christian antiquity, while understanding key concepts from the Calvinist Reformation. One of the most striking features of *The Primer* is its provision of set prayers. After all, Owen wrote at length in other publications against the use of set prayers, especially in the liturgy of the established church, and he always defended his claim that in public worship all addresses to God should be extemporaneous.[31] In providing children with set forms for daily prayer, Owen was recognizing the difference between private and public worship, as well as the difference between what might be expected of adult worshipers and what might be expected of children who were learning the Christian faith.

---

31. See, for example, his *Discourse concerning Liturgies* (1662).

The question was particularly acute in relation to the Lord's Prayer, for in encouraging children to use this traditional liturgical form, Owen was allowing children a spiritual routine that he would deny to their believing parents. In a later publication, Owen was clear that the Lord's Prayer was not appropriate for use in public worship, but it did provide a model for use in private worship.[32] His criticism of this liturgical tradition reflected his aspiration that public worship should be guided by the Holy Spirit. The guidance of the Spirit was still claimed by ministers within the Church of England, some of whom were breaking the law by continuing to use the recently proscribed Book of Common Prayer, and by ministers within the community of Presbyterians, who used as a liturgical form the Westminster Assembly's Directory for Public Worship. Yet Owen understood that extemporaneous worship would be facilitated by the Spirit. He argued that Jesus had provided his disciples with a formula for prayer to guide them in the period of time before his gift of the Spirit made such formulae redundant:

> Our Saviour at that time was minister of the circumcision, and taught the doctrine of the gospel under and with the observation of all the worship of the Judaical church. He was not yet glorified, and so the Spirit was not as yet given; I mean that Spirit which He promised unto His disciples to enable them to perform all the worship of God by Him required at their hands, whereof we have before spoken. That, then, which the Lord Jesus prescribed unto His disciples for their present practice in the worship of God, seems to have belonged unto the economy of the Old Testament. Now, to argue from the prescription of, and outward helps for, the performance of the worship of God under the Old Testament, unto a necessity of the like or the same under the

---

32. Owen, *Works*, 15:15.

New, is upon the matter to deny that Christ is ascended on high, and to have given spiritual gifts unto men eminently distinct from and above those given out by Him under the Judaical pedagogy.[33]

The Lord's Prayer, then, was suitable for Jewish believers before the giving of the Spirit and for the use of children in Christian families before their experience of saving grace and the consequent filling of the Spirit allowed for the possibility of extemporaneous worship.[34]

Owen's encouragement for children to use the Lord's Prayer threw up other anomalies. After all, he was encouraging children who had been baptized but who had not yet been incorporated into the church after a credible profession of faith to approach God as their Father. He made this position explicit in the morning and evening prayers. "A prayer for the morning" began by addressing the "Blessed Lord God, the God and Father of our Lord and Saviour Jesus Christ: and in him my God, and my Father," but it continued, with some uncertainty, to have the child pray that she might yet be made "accepted in thy beloved Son." Similarly, in one of the evening prayers, the supplicant requested, "Stretch out thy Fatherly armes unto my soule, to receive it with mercy into thy bosom [of] love," while the other appealed to "my dear Father in Jesus Christ."[35] Like his new friends among the Baptists, Owen was arguing that children should be regarded as being outside the boundaries of the church and the pale of salvation, but like his Congregational and Presbyterian colleagues, he insisted that they should still be able to address God as their Father.

---

33. Owen, *Works*, 15:14.

34. For a discussion of the relevance of Owen's views of the Lord's Prayer, see William Kelly, "Appendix to the Notice of the *Achill Herald* Recollections," *The Bible Treasury* 140 (1868): 15.

35. Owen, *The Primer*, n.p.

Owen faced up to the paradox, explaining that children using *The Primer* should be able to approach God as Father while simultaneously praying for their own salvation. He explained that "we come to have part and fellowship with Christ in the work of our redemption" by means of the "power of his Word and Spirit," through which we are "brought unto union with [Jesus Christ], and a participation of all the benefits by him purchased for us." Children should expect the Spirit to "quicken" them and to "beget" faith within them, which Owen described as a "grace of the Spirit" by which we "receive Jesus Christ for righteousnesse and salvation." Owen explained that the Spirit bestowed faith "in the preaching of the Word, confirming and increasing it, by the administration of the Sacraments." *The Primer* concluded with a review of the "chief benefits of the death of Christ," with definitions of *justification*, *adoption*, and *sanctification* slightly adapted from those of the Westminster Shorter Catechism, which were followed by the text of the Lord's Prayer and the Apostles' Creed.[36]

The brevity of this catechism is striking. Owen did not expect his "young learners" to grapple with complex or especially controversial theological ideas. *The Primer* attempted to simplify and abbreviate the content of the Shorter Catechism that had been prepared by the Westminster divines. Neither were the children of Christian families expected to understand much beyond the conviction that Scripture is the repository of "all truth concerning God, and our selves"; God as Trinity and Creator; the fall, the transmission of the original sin, and the sinner's "disability . . . to [do] any thing that is spiritually good"; the Ten Commandments as a record of the ways in which sinners fall short of God's glory; and God's provision of a way of salvation by grace through faith in Jesus Christ.

---

36. Owen, *The Primer*, n.p.

For all Owen's reputation as a champion of high Calvinism, the catechism he prepared for children made no mention of the divine decrees of election and reprobation or the extent or effect of the atonement. *The Primer* was focused on teaching children the central themes of the evangelical preaching that dominated mid-seventeenth-century England. The "young learners" using this book would know how to read and count and would understand basic ideas about God as Trinity, the creation of humanity, the fall, and redemption through Jesus Christ. They would be taught to pray, committing their days to their heavenly Father and thanking him for their food, and they would come to understand God's care of creation through learning Psalm 104, the incarnation through learning Matthew 2, and the atonement through learning John 18–19. The "young learners" who were taught from *The Primer* would understand the need for faith, while knowing that God was their Father.[37]

And the set prayers, too, were short. Owen did not have unrealistic expectations of the children whose faith he sought to nurture. They were infants, he might have considered, and their Christian formation had to pay attention to the limits of their comprehension and their attention span. But this was a signal of his high, not low, expectations of their potential. For growing up in a home suffused with prayer, a home that recognized God's blessing in everyday providences, and a home that returned thanks for it, the children who learned about their faith were in reality learning about their family and its world. The religious instruction of children was too important to be allocated only special time in a weekly routine. It had to happen everywhere, all the time, daily, hourly, individually at the close and break of day, and every time the family ate. The parents' piety and their hopes for their children created an atmosphere

---

37. Owen, *The Primer*, n.p.

in the home that their religious instruction explained and that the life of the church confirmed. And church services were to be organized to take account of the attention span of the little ones, as he elsewhere observed: "Better a great number should complain of the shortness of some duties . . . than that a few who are sincere should be really discouraged by being over-burdened, and have the service thereby made useless to them."[38] Owen's sense of the spiritual formation of children recognized the centrality of the family unit, even as it acknowledged that spiritual formation took a village—or at least, a village church.

Catechism

The Primer represented a simplification of the catechisms that Owen had prepared during his years of parish ministry in Essex villages. The material contained in *The Principles of the Doctrine of Christ, Unfolded in Two Short Catechismes* (1645) was supplementary to Owen's public ministry, and he excused his brief treatment of the sacraments because, he said, "I have already been so frequent in examinations about them."[39] He likewise recognized that he had "wholly omitted" any discussion of "moral duties," hoping at some later date to provide an exposition of the Lord's Prayer, the Ten Commandments, and the Apostles' Creed, an aspiration that he partially fulfilled in *The Primer*.[40]

The Principles of the Doctrine of Christ contained a "lesser catechism" that was to be learned by the "younger sort," which he expected to be taught in families.[41] While this catechism contained only thirty-three questions, it covered significant

---

38. Owen, *Works*, 19:458.
39. Owen, *Works*, 1:466.
40. Owen, *Works*, 1:466. William Goold, Owen's nineteenth-century editor, does not appear to have been aware of *The Primer* and believed that Owen never fulfilled this aspiration. Owen, *Works*, 1:464.
41. Owen, *Works*, 1:465.

doctrinal range and assumed that those who learned its contents had savingly benefited from its doctrine. After all, as we have just noted, in his early years of ministry Owen maintained a very high view of baptism. His "lesser catechism" described the "holy ordinance" as the sprinkling with water, "according to Christ's institution," whereby "we are by his grace made children of God, and have the promises of the covenants sealed unto us."[42] And so, beginning with the statement that "all truth concerning God and ourselves" is to be learned from Scripture, the catechism went on to consider the essence of God; his Trinitarian being; his decrees of election and reprobation; his works in creation and providence; the fall of our first parents; our deliverance through Jesus Christ; Christ's offices as prophet, priest, and king; Christ's humiliation and exaltation; and the claim that Christ performed his offices "only for his elect." The catechism described the "universal company of God's elect" as the church and recognized that members were added to the church "by a lively faith," an "assured resting of the soul upon God's promises of mercy in Jesus Christ, for pardon of sins here and glory hereafter." This faith is not the basis for our being accounted righteous, which comes "only for the righteousness of Christ, freely imputed unto us, and laid hold of by faith."[43] The Christian life requires "universal obedience to the will of God revealed unto us" and brings privileges, including union with Christ; our adoption into God's family; the fellowship that we share with other believers; a right to the seals of the new covenant, baptism, and the Lord's Supper; Christian liberty; and the hope of resurrection.[44]

As this shorter catechism demonstrated, Owen had high expectations of the "younger sort" and of the families that would

---

42. Owen, *Works*, 1:469.
43. Owen, *Works*, 1:468.
44. Owen, *Works*, 1:467–70.

teach them. The "greater catechism" offered a substantial exposition of the shorter text by turning almost every one of its questions into a "chapter" of questions in which the abstract designed for children could be more systematically explained. This longer catechism was prepared for those who would be instructing their families in the faith, and Owen insisted that those who used his work should take responsibility to test his theological statements against the biblical citations that he provided.

Owen prepared his "greater catechism" with a broader purpose. In 1645, the year of its publication, Parliament had passed an ordinance that radically restricted admission to the Lord's Supper. For centuries, the residents of England's eleven thousand parishes had been admitted to the Eucharist simply on the grounds of their location. This situation changed during the First English Civil War (1642–1646), when the party of Presbyterians then in the ascendant pushed for a tightening of expectations about the beliefs and behavior of those who should be admitted to the Table. The Presbyterians were reflecting widespread concerns that the English Reformation had been ineffective in its program of confessionalization. And so the ordinance required ministers to examine congregants regarding their faith and practice and to permit to the Lord's Supper only those who could demonstrate a credible profession of faith and a reasonable proficiency in Christian knowledge. Owen's "greater catechism" was one of a number of catechetical works to be published in 1645 to address this need. It was a handbook for pastoral practice, and it offered guidelines for the minimum level of doctrinal knowledge required of those who should be admitted into the church.

This catechism indicated what Owen believed could be achieved by the coordinated efforts of the family and the local church. He wanted his doctrinal preaching to be reinforced by doctrinal instruction in the home, as children worked from the "lesser catechism" to capture the more detailed account of the faith in the longer text. And the effect of this formal course of doctrinal instruction would be that Christian families could do more with the preaching they heard each Sunday. As the content of that preaching became easier to assimilate, so its potential increased as a means of grace. Doctrinal teaching in the home and in the church created a virtuous circle that energized growth in grace, which would be further enabled by admission into the fellowship of the church and to its means of grace, especially the Lord's Supper. Catechesis enabled entry to church fellowship, and it nurtured spiritual life.

Conclusion

Owen's account of Christian nurture pulled together the roles of the family and the church. He was convinced that children growing up in Christian homes and churches should be encouraged to believe that God was their Father. Owen expected Christian families to reinforce the teaching of the church by instructing their children in the three classical forms—the Lord's Prayer, the Ten Commandments, and the Apostles' Creed—as well as in the catechisms that he provided in the 1640s as a parish minister and in the 1650s as a public theologian with a day job in university administration. Owen's publications allowed for children to be gradually formed in their understanding of their Christian heritage. *The Primer* offers a glimpse into the simplicity he expected of childhood piety within the home, as well as the daily routines of thankfulness that he expected parents to exemplify. *The Principles of the Doctrine of Christ* offered a more technically demanding "lesser catechism" and a much more substantial "greater catechism," which must have challenged his parishioners in its detail and extent but which was designed to prepare them for life within the church. Taken together, these publications suggest how Owen hoped that those who consumed the "pure milk of the word" in childhood could be nurtured into capable theologians in adolescence and in preparation for admission into the congregation. It was the hope of one of the earliest of English children's writers that the "newborn babes" who "desire the sincere milk of the word" would so "grow thereby" (1 Pet. 2:2) as to be "no more children, tossed to and fro, and carried about with every wind of doctrine," but to be those who, "speaking the truth in love," would "grow up into him in all things, which is the head, even Christ" (Eph. 4:14–15), and would thus experience the grace that enables spiritual life.

2

Youth

In his early twenties, shortly after abandoning his plans for a university career, and perhaps during the long period of depression that predated his conversion, John Owen read a book that left a lasting impression on his mind. He must have borrowed this copy of Henry Scudder's *The Christians Daily Walk* (1627), which was one of the best-selling and most frequently reprinted Puritan devotional manuals, for he did not return to the work for another thirty years. When he did read the work for a second time, to prepare a commendatory preface for its eleventh edition, which appeared in 1674, his appreciation of Scudder's work had only increased.[1] In terms of method, Scudder expressed himself "not . . . with enticing words of mans wisdom, nor in profound Scholastical reasonings, but in an evident deduction of all his useful Directions from express testimonies of Scripture."[2] In terms of argument, Scudder's goal, which so profoundly affected Owen,

---

1. John Owen, "Dr. Owen to the Reader," in Henry Scudder, *The Christians Daily Walk* (London, 1674), sig. Ar.
2. Owen, "To the Reader," in Scudder, *Christians Daily Walk*, sig. A2r.

was to recommend to his readers "such a walking with God . . . that we may come to the enjoyment of him hereafter."[3] *The Christians Daily Walk* offered Owen a devotional tool to nurture spiritual life.

Owen's recollection of the impact of Scudder's work provided him with tools for his own preaching to young adults. For if Owen's theology of childhood was focused on initiation, nurture, and theological instruction, in ministering to young people he emphasized the same issues of piety and spirituality that he had found so affecting in *The Christians Daily Walk*. While speaking to and writing for young people, Owen, like Scudder, abandoned the habits of scholastic theology, drawing on texts "as I find them lying scattered up and down in the Scripture," without "casting them into any artificial method."[4] The fruit of Owen's ministry to young adults was the reimagined and reenergized Calvinism that shaped his most enduring literary contributions.

Owen had occasion to think carefully about the spiritual needs of young people, for during the 1650s, he spent much of his ministry preaching to Oxford undergraduates. Enrollment was at its peak in the early seventeenth century, when matriculations at England's two universities suddenly expanded. Many of those to whom Owen preached would have been in their mid- to late teens. Their experience would have corresponded to his own, for, little more than three decades previously, Owen had arrived in Oxford at age twelve, along with his slightly older brother, to begin undergraduate studies. He appears to have been an active and energetic young man, who, one of his friends recalled, enjoyed athletics and other sports but who was also intensely serious about his studies. It was during this period that Owen established a sustained habit of sleeping for around four

---

3. Owen, "To the Reader," in Scudder, *Christians Daily Walk*, sig. Av.
4. Owen, *Works*, 2:235.

hours each night. His pattern of sleep was part of a self-imposed disciplinary regime that was enabled by diligent time management and that facilitated his "greediness of study."[5]

Owen worked hard at his studies. He remembered what it was to "study with all diligence day and night."[6] Sometimes he found his studies challenging, as when he worked with difficulty through Aristotle. At other times he found his initiation into the classics rewarding and even moving, as in his discovery of Homer.[7] These writers guided his thinking across disciplines: his earliest publications constructed central themes in Reformed theology by drawing on the writers of classical antiquity, who were footnoted in his early theological writings almost as often as the best-known names in the Western theological canon. Owen was certainly bookish. It may have been during these teenage years that he began to collect the first volumes of the library that would expand by the time of his death to include more than three thousand (mainly theological) items.[8] For books were weapons in Owen's Oxford, where the achievements of Protestantism were suddenly up for debate. His formation in the classics took place in the context of a bitter theological contest, as his teachers in the Queen's College divided between those who favored the teaching established during the English Reformation and those who preferred the liturgical innovations that had been introduced by the university's new chancellor, the recently appointed bishop of London, and future archbishop of Canterbury, William Laud. This division was attended by at least the threat of violence among the fellows of the Queen's

5. Owen, *Works*, 6:44.
6. Owen, *Works*, 6:119.
7. Owen, *Works*, 10:49, 50.
8. See Edward Millington, *Bibliotheca Oweniana* (London, 1684), for a purported record of the content of Owen's library.

College. It was a dangerous—and stimulating—time to pursue a theological education.

But although Owen found his Oxford education intellectually fulfilling, it did not address what was coming to be his deepest spiritual concern. After completing his undergraduate studies, Owen decided to abandon his university career, since he could not sign on to the Laudian innovations in the university, which, as a prospective academic, he would have to approve. This decision was made on grounds of principle but before he had come fully to internalize the theology for which he was willing to take such extraordinary personal risk. Even before his conversion, in his early twenties, Owen was willing to make a sacrificial commitment to Reformed theology. His theological learning had not driven him to a personal experience of conversion, but his costly decision in defense of his theological conclusions may have done so: later in life, he remembered that "a despising of all things for Christ is the very first lesson of the gospel."[9] And further lessons in the gospel were to follow. Leaving the university for a precarious situation in the capital, Owen was converted, not through the teaching of Oxford fellows but through the ministry of an unknown preacher standing in at short notice for one of London's pulpit celebrities. Owen's university experience was in some sense a missed opportunity. For all his learning, his greatest discovery was not an idea but an experience. Owen's new birth and early spiritual formation took place in cheap lodgings in London and with the help of a borrowed book.

And so, while Owen certainly prized the life of the mind, he was fully aware of the limitations of doctrinal knowledge. "Empty professors" could easily be mistaken for "saints," he worried, in a sermon addressed to Oxford undergradu-

---

9. Owen, *Works*, 2:137.

ates; "fruitless professors often walk hand in hand" with the godly in the "performance of duties, and . . . the enjoyment of outward privileges." But "now come to their secret retirements, and what a difference is there! There saints hold communion with God: hypocrites, for the most part, with the world and their own lusts."[10] Any child could be catechized, and any academic could make sacrificial decisions for the sake of principle, he realized, but only saints could grow in grace: "That knowledge of God . . . which we have by the word, the letter of it . . . is not saving to us if we have no other help," for "there is a wide difference between understanding the doctrine of Scripture as in the letter, and a true knowing the mind of Christ."[11] He concluded that the difference between true Christians and those who merely imitated the life of faith could be found in their affections. Echoing the title of Scudder's work *The Christians Daily Walk*, Owen observed that the "daily walk" of believers should have the purpose of getting "their hearts crucified to the world and the things of it, and the world to their hearts; that they may not have living affections to dying things."[12] For intellectual assent to orthodox doctrinal propositions and an external forsaking of sin were not sufficient for salvation. Those whose emotions were not engaged with the theology they studied would "readily change truth for error."[13]

Oxford had shown Owen that anyone could become a theologian. But his experience in London had persuaded him that true believers could be distinguished from false professors—and that true believers were distinguished not by what they knew but by how that knowledge made them feel and by what those

---

10. Owen, *Works*, 2:39.
11. Owen, *Works*, 2:108, 120.
12. Owen, *Works*, 2:150.
13. Owen, *Works*, 2:248.

affections made them do. An emotional and volitional response to the gospel was critically important. True conversion involved the will and the heart as well as the mind, and Owen's ministry to students targeted those whose knowledge of the gospel was merely intellectual.

Owen's Return to Oxford

Owen was a changed man when he returned to Oxford in 1651. After several years of parish ministry, the cultivation of several well-placed patrons, and an army chaplaincy during the invasions of Ireland and Scotland, Owen reentered academic life around the age of thirty-five. He was still young enough to remember the experience of youth, the dizzying possibilities of learning, and the sense that there was more to read than there could ever be time to read it. And so, as he began his career as a professor of theology and a university administrator, Owen took opportunities to speak to undergraduates about the things that he believed should matter most. As dean of Christ Church from 1651 and as vice-chancellor of the university from 1652, Owen made strenuous efforts to inspire his young charges with a vision of godliness enabled by the Calvinism that he was beginning to reimagine.

Owen's new surroundings were very familiar—and so was the life of his students. He was quite aware of their potential for disruptive and occasionally riotous behavior. As college dean and university vice-chancellor, he sat on committees that considered breaches of student discipline, some of which were serious indeed. He did his best to calm the graduation ceremonies, in which students had engaged in a carnivalesque inversion of academic hierarchies and in which their behavior had spun out of control. His agenda for university reform included the pastoral care of his undergraduates, which he advanced in his teaching and preaching.

Owen took education very seriously and understood its purpose in redemptive terms. Like John Milton, Samuel Hartlib, and other Protestant pedagogical theorists, he argued that education was meant to be restorative. In a book that was based on sermons he had preached to the university community, Owen explained that Adam, in Eden, had been given an almost "perfect" knowledge of the divine will and created order.[14] But this knowledge had been reduced after his expulsion from the garden, and it had been further dissipated by means of the division of tongues at Babel. The effect of this sudden eclipse of knowledge had been social as well as religious:

> Ignorance, darkness, and blindness, is come upon the understanding; acquaintance with the works of God, spiritual and natural, is lost; strangeness of communication is given, by multiplication of tongues; tumultuating of passions and affections, with innumerable darkening prejudices, are also come upon us.

Education was about unpicking knots, he explained in a central, extended metaphor. The "whole design of learning" was to "disentangle the soul" from the effects of sin; or, as he put it more fully, the "aim and tendency of literature" was to "disentangle the mind in its reasonings, to recover an acquaintance with the works of God, to subduct the soul from under the effects of the curse of division of tongues." Learning was a means to recover lost knowledge, the "particular end" of which was to "remove some part of that curse which is come upon us by sin."[15] Education was to "recover" the knowledge that was lost in the fall in order to help Christians in their "walking with God."[16] In its ideal form, education was meant to be redemptive, an enabler of the spiritual life.

---

14. Owen, *Works*, 2:112.
15. Owen, *Works*, 2:112.
16. Owen, *Works*, 2:113.

But, Owen recognized, education could not now fulfill this redemptive purpose, for the fall had affected the human mind as well as the heart and the will. And so, for all their "profound inquiries . . . subtle disputations . . . acute reasonings [and] admirable discoveries," Socrates, Plato, Aristotle, and the other writers of antiquity had become "fools" in what mattered most.[17] An individual who "attained the greatest height of literature . . . if he have not Christ, is as much under the curse of blindness, ignorance, stupidity, dullness, as the poorest, silliest soul in the world," Owen lamented, for "the utmost that man's wisdom can do, is but to find out the most wretched, burdensome, and vexatious ways of perishing eternally."[18] "Learning is the product of the soul's struggling with the curse for sin," he recognized, but it could do little to alleviate the suffering of the world without the light of the gospel.[19] And so, he later explained, the "praise of Gods grace" ought to be the "end of all our Writing and Reading."[20] Education could not achieve its redemptive purpose without grace—without the gospel.

Owen's efforts at reforming the student body met with mixed success. His college community was home to many gifted students, including some who would be among the most famous names in the cultural life of the later seventeenth century. Some students in Christ Church, including John Locke, the future philosopher, did not appreciate Owen's program for their improvement; in letters to acquaintances, Locke made fun of his college dean. The resistance of other students was more overt: on at least one occasion, a large party from Christ Church invaded another college and wreaked havoc.

---

17. Owen, *Works*, 2:113.
18. Owen, *Works*, 2:105, 114.
19. Owen, *Works*, 2:112.
20. Owen, "To the Reader," in Scudder, *Christians Daily Walk*, sig. A2r.

But some individuals within the academic community did appreciate Owen's efforts for their good. Many serious-minded undergraduates responded positively to his call to godliness and were impressed by the spiritual atmosphere that Owen encouraged as he appealed to the students to walk with Christ.[21] One such student kept notes of Owen's preaching, which show how his emphases were being reinforced by the preaching of his colleagues in and beyond the university. Thomas Aldersey matriculated in Brasenose College in 1653, when Owen's influence was at its height and when his reform of the university was pushing forward. Like many other earnest young Puritans, Aldersey, then in his late teens, kept notebooks that recorded the sermons he attended for the first two years of his undergraduate career. Puritan devotional writers had encouraged this practice, hoping that notetaking would encourage greater attention during preaching and greater retention of its content afterward. These notes, which have never been considered in any account of this period in Owen's life, show how students were encouraged by Owen's work, just as he had been encouraged by Henry Scudder to abandon the scholastic approach of the university theology in favor of serious Bible study and the pursuit of the knowledge of God.[22]

Aldersey's notebooks offer a rare glimpse into the kinds of preaching that the Oxford students could hear. In his first year of studies, Aldersey was attending sermons by a range of preachers, including Oxford academics such as the two Henry Wilkinsons, respectively the canon of Christ Church and principal of Magdalene Hall; John Wilkins, warden of Wadham College; and the Presbyterian minister and Westminster Assembly member Edward Reynolds. While they were all sympathetic

---

21. For examples of Owen's invitational method, see Owen, *Works*, 6:523; 10:300.
22. Owen, "To the Reader," in Scudder, *Christians Daily Walk*, sig. Av.

to the theology and piety of the Calvinist Reformation, they had very different views of church order, came from different sides in Oxford's culture war, and nursed personal rivalries to boot. Reynolds, for example, had been dean of Christ Church until he had been ousted by a committee that wished to appoint Owen in his place, and Reynolds in turn would replace Owen after he fell out of favor with the Cromwell family at the end of the decade. Despite these sometimes serious differences, these men shared a common outlook on Christian faith and behavior—but, as Aldersey's notebooks suggest, not many of them were able to present Reformed theology with Owen's imagination.

Owen's Reimagined Calvinism

Aldersey's notebooks show how Owen preached through material that found its way into his later published works. His sermon on Romans 8:13, for example, which included the assertion that "life depends upon mortification," was recycled in *Of the Mortification of Sin in Believers* (1656).[23] This pithy paradox—that spiritual life depends on death—shows how Owen was not content merely to restate familiar doctrines in familiar ways in his preaching to undergraduates. His addresses to students provided the context for some of his most significant theological work. In 1651, he delivered a series of sermons in St. Mary's, Oxford, outlining how the doctrine of the Trinity could facilitate a new kind of spirituality. Drawing on the benediction recorded in 2 Corinthians 13:14, Owen argued that believers could have fellowship with each person of the Godhead in distinct ways, so that "our peculiar communion [is] with the Father in love, the Son in grace, and the Holy Ghost in consolation."[24] This proved

---

23. Notebook of Thomas Aldersey, Oxford, Bodleian Library, MS Don. f. 40, fol. 113r.

24. Owen, *Works*, 2:228.

to be a controversial claim, and it became the subject of censure. Some listeners encouraged Owen to publish the sermons, but he took time to think through the consequences of his arguments and the substance of the criticisms that they had received.[25] All the while, as Aldersey's notes attest, Owen continued to reflect in his public preaching on the possibility of communion with God.

Aldersey heard Owen preach on several occasions in spring 1653. He took extended notes on several discourses, including one on John 21:20.[26] This was a useful text for Owen to reflect on. It provided the base for his discussion of the principal duties of pastors in his posthumously published study *The True Nature of a Gospel Church* (1689). In that work, the writing of which cannot be reliably dated in his career, Owen explained that the principal duties of pastors included feeding the flock through diligent preaching, which should reflect spiritual wisdom, personal experience of the power of truth, competence in hermeneutics, zeal for God's glory, compassion for the souls of those being addressed, and an awareness of their particular needs. In the same season, Aldersey took notes on another sermon, on 1 John 1:3, which showed how Owen was following his own advice and which would come to provide the introduction for his classic work of Puritan spirituality, *Of Communion with God* (1657).

Owen was making these claims about communion with each divine person at the same time that Trinitarian theology was becoming a subject of political debate and that influential voices were proposing alternatives to the historical doctrine of the church. Senior government figures had become alarmed by what they understood to be the sudden popularity

---

25. Owen, *Works*, 2:2–3; Sarah Gibbard Cook, "A Political Biography of a Religious Independent: John Owen, 1616–1683" (PhD diss., Harvard University, 1972), 240–41.
26. Notebook of Thomas Aldersey, Oxford, Bodleian Library, MS Don. f. 38 fols. 75v–77v, 115v–117v.

of Socinianism and by the increasing number of publications promoting varieties of the non-Trinitarian theology that had developed in post-Reformation Poland. Owen was drawn into these debates and was asked to prepare a book in defense of the Western catholic tradition. He published the results of his study as *Vindiciae Evangelicae* (1655).[27] He was only too aware that his students faced intellectual temptations: in 1656, he worried that Oxford undergraduates were reading Hugo Grotius, whose approach to studying religion he believed corrosive of Reformed orthodoxy.[28] But these temptations were not to be met by a simple restatement of established dogmatic conclusions.

Owen recognized that the biggest threat to his promotion of true religion was a scholastic Calvinism that touched the mind but not the heart or will. This unbalanced application of biblical theology led to unbiblical emphases, he feared, and fatally distorted the doctrine of God. He regretted that so many of his contemporaries thought of God as being "hard, austere, severe, almost implacable, and fierce."[29] He feared that these individuals "fix their thoughts only on his terrible majesty, severity and greatness; and so their spirits are not endeared."[30] Their misunderstanding of the character of God was—literally—fatal.

So Owen determined to find a way around this distorted theology. In his sermons and lectures on "communion with God," he drew on the famous introduction to Calvin's *Institutes of the Christian Religion* (1559) to argue that "the sum of all true wisdom and knowledge" should "be reduced to these

27. Philip Dixon, *Nice and Hot Disputes: The Doctrine of the Trinity in the Seventeenth Century* (London: T&T Clark, 2003), 34–65; Sarah Mortimer, *Reason and Religion in the English Revolution: The Challenge of Socinianism*, Cambridge Studies in Early Modern British History (Cambridge: Cambridge University Press, 2010), 196–212.

28. Owen, *Works*, 12:619.

29. Owen, *Works*, 2:35.

30. Owen, *Works*, 2:32.

three heads": "the knowledge of God, his nature and his properties," "the knowledge of ourselves in reference to the will of
God concerning us," and, he added to the contribution of his
more famous predecessor, "skill to walk in communion with
God."[31] Owen's work was to train up his students in the way
that they should go, preparing them for church membership by
teaching them, as Calvin had put it, how to know God, how
to walk with God, and how to understand themselves. And
this he did in one of the most remarkable proposals in early
modern theology and spirituality, preaching and then publishing sermons that, as one recent commentator put it, "exploited
underdeveloped and latent allowances in the tradition" even as
it "stretched the limits of then current Augustinian assumptions
about the unity of the Godhead."[32] *Of Communion with God*
drew on Owen's massive biblical and theological learning to
expand on the Western Trinitarian consensus by arguing that
Christians could and should cultivate distinct relationships with
each of the divine persons. And so, six years after his sermons
on the subject were first delivered, Owen published his greatest
and most important and enduring contribution to evangelical
literature, *Of Communion with God*.

Knowing God

As an introduction to Owen's high Calvinism, *Of Communion
with God* must have been startling. The book was "designed
for popular edification," as he later explained, "accommodated
unto a popular way of instruction," and it sought to provide
a study of spirituality informed by the theology that resonated
with the concerns of the undergraduates who were listening

---

31. Owen, *Works*, 2:80.
32. Brian K. Kay, *Trinitarian Spirituality: John Owen and the Doctrine of God in
Western Devotion*, Studies in Christian History and Thought (Milton Keynes, UK: Paternoster, 2007), 6–7.

to his preaching.[33] In his published sermons, Owen addressed his student audience directly. He understood the reality of peer pressure, frankly admitting the "disadvantages" faced by students who pursued an active spiritual life, but he sought to balance this with an inspiring and innovative account of the kinds of communion that believers could enjoy with the Father, Son, and Holy Spirit.[34] He remembered, perhaps thinking of the stereotypes represented by William Shakespeare's Malvolio and Ben Jonson's Zeal-of-the-Land Busy, that those who earnestly pursued the spiritual life had been "the object of scorn and reproach from all sorts of men, from the pulpit to the stage."[35] Speaking to students, Owen said, for you who "are yet in the flower of your days, full of health and strength," the divine persons are "a fit object for your choicest affections."[36]

Owen's meditation was centered on the incarnate Son, who reveals the Father and sends the Spirit. Drawing on Revelation 3:20, Owen imagined Jesus's wooing of the lost soul:

> Behold, he stands at the door of your souls, and knocks: O reject him not, lest you seek him and find him not! Pray study him a little; you love him not, because you know him not. Why doth one of you spend his time in idleness and folly, and wasting of precious time—perhaps debauchedly? Why doth another associate and assemble himself with them that scoff at religion and the things of God? Merely because you know not our dear Lord Jesus.[37]

Throughout the book, as in this instance, Owen's argument was focused not on scholastic distinctions or theological minutiae

---

33. Owen, *Works*, 2:277, 330.
34. Owen, *Works*, 2:5.
35. Owen, *Works*, 2:255.
36. Owen, *Works*, 2:53.
37. Owen, *Works*, 2:53.

but on the test of spiritual experience, emphasizing not only the sovereignty of God but also the responsibility of those to whom the gospel call was addressed.

Of Communion with God was logically organized, and after discussing fellowship with the Father, Owen presented a longer discussion of fellowship with the Son and a much briefer account of fellowship with the Spirit. Owen appealed to the affections of his readers and sustained this appeal by developing an extended metaphor that reflected historic discussions of God, which he pressed into new kinds of service.[38] For many centuries before this point, Christian theologians had conceived of God as a fountain, drawing on passages like Zechariah 13:1, which Owen cited.[39] Owen pushed this metaphor to the center of his work.

Owen's use of this imagery was rooted in his discussion of the Father, whom he described as the "fountain of the Deity," and thus he provided an overview of the plan of salvation from the Father's perspective.[40] Owen argued that the "great discovery of the gospel" was the astonishing revelation that the Father is love.[41] And so he began his description of the believer's communion with the Father by quoting 1 John 4:8, "God is love," and by emphasizing that the Father's love came before the voluntary incarnation of the Son. For the Father's initiative was integral to salvation: it was the Father's declaration about the Son that provided the basis for the believer's recognition of the Son as Savior, so that saving faith was as much fixed on the Father's testimony concerning the Son as it was on the work of the Lord Jesus Christ himself.[42] And so,

---

38. Owen, *Works*, 2:34.
39. Owen, *Works*, 2:203.
40. Owen, *Works*, 2:13.
41. Owen, *Works*, 2:19.
42. Owen, *Works*, 2:13.

just as the Father is the "fountain of the Deity," the "great fountain and spring of all gracious communications and fruits of love," and the fountain of answers to prayer, so his love was to be recognized as the "fountain of all following gracious dispensations."[43] Christ's work on the cross did not compel the Father's love for believers: "The eternal love of the Father is not the fruit but the fountain of his purchase."[44]

Owen extended the imagery of the divine fountain to the Son. If the Father is the "fountain, this sun of eternal love itself," then Jesus Christ is "the beam, the stream," who leads us to his source.[45] This is why Bible writers drew on familiar images of love and care to portray the Father as "a mother, a shepherd, a hen over chickens, and the like."[46] Owen described the Father as demonstrating "delight and joy" in his people. Drawing on Zephaniah 3:17, he pictured the Father as leaping, "like a man overcome with some joyful surprisal," as he "sings to his church."[47] And Christians, too, should "leap for joy."[48] For Christ, he argued, is the "fountain of grace and mercy," in whom there is grace sufficient for "millions of worlds . . . because [his love] flows . . . from an infinite, bottomless fountain."[49] Christ is an "endless, bottomless fountain of grace to all them that believe."[50] "The life and soul of all our comforts lie treasured up in the promises of Christ," whose affirmation of the promises shows us what the Father is like.[51] And communion with the Son would change what believers are like: "One moment's communion with Christ by faith . . .

---

43. Owen, *Works*, 2:21, 23, 124, 228.
44. Owen, *Works*, 2:198.
45. Owen, *Works*, 2:23.
46. Owen, *Works*, 2:22.
47. Owen, *Works*, 2:25.
48. Owen, *Works*, 2:33.
49. Owen, *Works*, 2:62.
50. Owen, *Works*, 2:68.
51. Owen, *Works*, 2:239.

is more effective to the purging of the soul, to the increasing of grace, than the utmost self-endeavours of a thousand ages."[52] The Son was the fountain of our knowledge of God but also, in the glory of his resurrection humanity, the promise of what believers would one day become.

Owen also applied the image of the fountain to the person and work of the Spirit.[53] He depicted the Spirit as a "well of water springing up in the soul," providing "refreshment" in the life of holiness, and as "the fountain of that purchased grace wherein the saints have communion with Christ."[54] The Spirit "secretly infuseth and distils [joy] into the soul, prevailing against all fears and sorrows, filling it with gladness, exultations; and sometimes with unspeakable raptures of mind."[55] Owen allowed for almost ecstatic experiences of communion with God, as his imagery of the divine fountain spilled over into his description of the delights of the Christian life, and the adoption into God's family that is "our great and fountain privilege."[56] In the gospel is "a fountain opened," he argued, for in communion with the Father, Son, and Spirit, the believer would have "all things in the fountain, which others have but in the drops."[57]

Despite its creativity, rhetorical invention, and rich descriptive style, *Of Communion with God* never deviated from its high Calvinist roots. Owen's emphasis on religious affections did not dilute his theology; it merely provided his doctrinal arguments with a new range of imagery from which to draw and subtler means to make familiar points. The Father loves believers, Owen insisted, and his observation that "loving is

---

52. Owen, *Works*, 2:204.
53. Owen, *Works*, 2:226.
54. Owen, *Works*, 2:169, 252.
55. Owen, *Works*, 2:253.
56. Owen, *Works*, 2:207.
57. Owen, *Works*, 2:38, 204.

choosing" was his glance toward the Calvinist doctrine of un-conditional election: the delights of the relationship that he was describing were available only to some.[58] He similarly reframed the debate about the doctrine of total depravity: there was no reason why the Father's love should be universally extended, he continued, for while "we have all cause in the world to love him," the Father "loves us without a cause that is in ourselves," and his love "goes not only before our love, but also [before] any thing in us that is lovely."[59] And affirming the doctrine of the perseverance of the saints, Owen insisted that from the "fountain" of love "proceeds everything that is lovely in its object."[60] The Father's love "cannot be heightened by any act of ours" and "cannot be lessened by any thing in us," for "God loves his people in their sinning."[61] And in the security of that position, the enjoyment of divine love was to be the foundation of piety, as "the soul gathers itself from all its wanderings, from all other beloveds, to rest in God alone."[62] In delighting in the love of the Father, the grace of the Son, and the fellowship of the Spirit, the believer goes from faith to faith and from grace to glory in the experience of spiritual life.

Conclusion

Owen's reading of Scudder's *The Christians Daily Walk* had given him a new view of the possibilities of Reformed theology in his early twenties. Almost two decades later, he took the op-portunity to reimagine his high Calvinism for an audience of undergraduates in sermons that reflected his "sometimes . . . unspeakable raptures of mind."[63] For Owen, the gospel was

---

58. Owen, *Works*, 2:28.
59. Owen, *Works*, 2:29, 37.
60. Owen, *Works*, 2:28.
61. Owen, *Works*, 2:30.
62. Owen, *Works*, 2:26.
63. Owen, *Works*, 2:253.

extraordinary, and his description of its central themes could border on the sublime:

> To see, indeed, a world made good and beautiful, wrapped up in wrath and curses, clothed with thorns and briers; to see the whole beautiful creation made subject to vanity, given up to the bondage of corruption; to hear it groan in pain under that burden; to consider legions of angels, most glorious and immortal creatures, cast down into hell, bound with chains of darkness, and reserved for a more dreadful judgment for one sin; to view the ocean of the blood of souls spilt to eternity on this account,—will give some insight into this thing. But what is all this to that view of it which may be had by a spiritual eye in the Lord Christ? . . . To see him who is the wisdom of God, and the power of God, always beloved of the Father; to see him, I say, fear, and tremble, and bow, and sweat, and pray, and die; to see him lifted up upon the cross, the earth trembling under him, as if unable to bear his weight; and the heavens darkened over him, as if shut against his cry; and himself hanging between both, as if refused by both; and all this because our sins did meet upon him;—this of all things doth most abundantly manifest the severity of God's vindictive justice. Here, or nowhere, is it to be learned.[64]

In exhortations like this, Owen's preaching to students moved beyond an emphasis on mind and will in an effort to engage their affections. The communion with God he recommended would drive the authentic spiritual experience that would provide a taste of heaven on earth. "The things wherein we have communion with Christ," taken up to "perfection," would be the substance of "everlasting glory," he insisted;

---

64. Owen, *Works*, 2:85.

"perfect acceptance, perfect holiness, perfect adoption, or in-heritance of sons,—that is glory."[65] Owen understood his tradi-tion. His preaching to young adults drew explicitly on Calvin's *Institutes*, in remembering that "the sum of all true wisdom and knowledge" could be reduced to "the knowledge of God, his nature and his properties" and "the knowledge of ourselves in reference to the will of God concerning us." But it was Owen's addition to this list—his emphasis on "skill to walk in com-munion with God," the lesson he had learned from Henry Scudder—that lay at the heart of his reforming of Reformed theology, inviting his undergraduate listeners into a spiritual life that would make a practical contribution in this world and reach its joyful conclusion in everlasting glory.[66]

65. Owen, *Works*, 2:173.
66. Owen, *Works*, 2:80.

Middle Age

Owen understood that communion with God, for all its almost ecstatic joys, was to be experienced in an often hostile world. By the 1660s, he had become very aware of the vicissitudes of the Christian life. In the previous decade, he had risen from obscurity to become England's leading public theologian and the vice-chancellor of the University of Oxford, before the rapidly changing circumstances of the Restoration required him to disappear from public view at an even greater speed.

The new political environment was shocking. After the implosion of the republic and the chaos that preceded the ensuing change of regime, the public mood turned violently against those it identified with the revolution and its unpopular attempts at cultural, legal, and moral reform. In 1660–1661, members of the Cavalier Parliament, lashing out with fury at those they deemed responsible for the personal and national disasters of the republic, pursued the leaders and defenders of the Cromwellian regime with bitter purpose. In the Act of Oblivion (1660), Charles protected from prosecution almost all those who had fought on the side of Parliament, except the men who had signed his father's death warrant, but politicians in his new government had a more ambitious view of who should be held to account for the excesses of the previous decade. As the list expanded, government agents pursued their targets in locations as far apart as Switzerland and New England. Those who were not fortunate enough to escape suffered in horrific spectacles of torture and execution, their heads and limbs being publicly displayed in London until the 1680s. Those who had once been allies were divided. Robert Baillie, the Scottish Covenanter leader and member of the Westminster Assembly, thought the restored regime to be executing the "justice of God" in putting the regicides to a "shamefull death," and in putting "to disgrace . . . the two Goodwins [Thomas and John Goodwin], blind Milton, Owen, Sterrie, Lockier, and others of that maleficent crew."[1] The wave of executions was followed by the imposition of a raft of new laws, known collectively as the Clarendon Code (1661–1665), which required universal conformity to the reestablished Church of England, creating a new community of dissenters and simultaneously proscribing the practice of their faith. The Restoration unwound the revolution. For the second time in a dozen years, England had been turned upside down.

Owen was in his mid-forties when the world as he knew it came to an end. For the previous fifteen years, he had pinned his hopes for the prosperity of the nation and for advancement in his own career on the success of a regime that had suddenly ceased to exist. His years of service to the republican government were now a political liability. Later in the decade, he claimed not to have been surprised by the outbreak of religious persecution that accompanied the collapse of the

---

1. Robert Baillie, *The Letters and Journals of Robert Baillie, 1637–1662*, ed. David Laing (Edinburgh: Robert Ogle, 1841–1842), 3:441.

republic and the restoration of monarchy. Scripture had "fully forewarned" the godly of these unexpected turns, he noted, "that so we might not at any time think ourselves surprised, as though some strange thing happened to us."[2] And, he added, "whatever disadvantages . . . we may be exposed unto, we have no reason to complain or think strange of, it being no other than all men in the like condition, in all ages, have had to conflict withal, and will have so whilst sin and darkness continue in the world."[3] But he must have been frightened. He remained in hiding through much of the first half of the decade, living with his wife and often apart from their youngest children, who remained in the care of friends.

Owen found consolation in his theological convictions and resisted tempting opportunities to conform. In 1664, Edward Hyde, the Earl of Clarendon, offered him a shortcut to family stability, financial security, and social respectability in the form of a bishopric within the established church.[4] But Owen, true to his reputation as the "Atlas of the Independents," stuck to his theological guns.[5] He faced up to the realities of religious persecution but insisted that these difficulties be providentially understood. He encouraged his co-religionists to see the collapse of Puritan government as occurring under the sovereign hand of God and to respond to these changing events in faith rather than in fear:

> What shall befall us in the course of our pilgrimage, how we shall be disposed of as to our outward temporary concernments, as it is not in our power to order and determine, so

---

2. Owen, *Works*, 13:544.

3. Owen, *Works*, 13:547.

4. Paul Seaward, *The Cavalier Parliament and the Reconstruction of the Old Regime, 1661–1667*, Cambridge Studies in Early Modern British History (Cambridge: Cambridge University Press, 1989), 29, 192, 318.

5. Anthony à Wood, *Athenae Oxonienses* (Oxford, 1813), 4:98.

> neither ought it to be in our care, so as that we should be
> anxiously solicitous thereabout: all things of that nature
> belong unto his sovereign pleasure, who will make them
> work together for good to them that love him.[6]

Owen understood that God was sovereign over the persecution of dissenters—and even over the bloody and spectacular revenge that had been wreaked on his friends. For, he insisted, drawing on Romans 8:28, God would certainly turn this suffering to good; as he put it in a sermon in 1673, "God keeps alive a little sparke in an Ocean."[7]

As the repressive measures of the Clarendon Code began to expire, Owen spent the second half of the decade thinking about the legal status of Protestant dissenters. He enjoyed the protection of a number of well-connected aristocrats and met frequently with the Earl of Clarendon, the often sympathetic administrator after whom the measures for religious repression had been misnamed. Owen thus began to hope that the king's enthusiasm to secure toleration for Roman Catholics, in a measure known as an "indulgence," might also benefit Presbyterians, Congregationalists, and Baptists.[8] Taking advantage of increasing freedom but still preferring anonymity, Owen published *A Brief Instruction in the Worship of God* (1667), which defined his aspiration for local church life. He also thought carefully about how dissenters might contribute to the greater good of society.

In a sequence of publications, from 1667 to 1670, Owen reiterated his religious convictions and constructed a political philosophy that made sense of that theological position in the very different circumstances of defeat, as a guide to the respon-

---

6. Owen, *Works*, 13:543.
7. Notebook of Lucy Hutchinson, DD/HU3, 232, Inspire Nottinghamshire Archives.
8. Seaward, *Cavalier Parliament*, 318.

sibilities of the Christian in the world and to the economic and political concerns that marked his middle age. In this period, Owen's argument for religious toleration—and for the kind of economic and political arrangements that would guarantee it—took its familiar form in the work of his most famous former student. For it was a Christ Church graduate who constructed the political philosophy that emerged from Owen's political theory, developing the classical liberalism through which his ideas have most powerfully shaped our world. Owen understood that "knowing God" involved supporting "the cause of the poor and needy" (Jer. 22:16). For Owen, and for those who adopted his arguments, dissenters had a responsibility to consider the political and social contribution that was concomitant of spiritual life.

Toleration and Politics

Owen's arguments about political principles became influential in the literary culture in which the best-known intervention was *An Essay concerning Toleration* (1667). In this work, John Locke channeled the arguments of his former college dean, though it would take the younger man a further decade and more to come to fully share Owen's ideals, as Locke would express them in his works on the religious settlement of the Glorious Revolution (1688–1690).[9]

Locke had been thinking about the ideal of religious toleration for some time. In Cromwellian Oxford, the idea had been much in the air. Henry Stubbe, Owen's Christ Church colleague and occasional research assistant, reported that the group of students that had arrived in the college from Westminster

---

9. For a discussion of the relationship between Owen and Locke, see Manfred Svensson, "John Owen and John Locke: Confessionalism, Doctrinal Minimalism, and Toleration," *History of European Ideas* 43, no. 4 (2017): 302–16; Robert Louis Wilken, *Liberty in the Things of God: The Christian Origins of Religious Freedom* (New Haven, CT: Yale University Press, 2019), 155–61.

School—among whom Locke would have been numbered—were "Dr Owen's creatures" and supporters of his notion of liberty of conscience.[10] Stubbe and Locke were certainly discussing the issue. In 1659, Locke wrote to the older man to observe how "men of different persuasions may quietly unite under the same government and unanimously carry the same civil interest, and hand in hand march to the same end of peace and mutual society, though they take different ways toward heaven."[11] Locke's assurance of the benefits of religious toleration were shaken after the Restoration, not least in his *First Tract on Government* (1660), when, like Owen and Stubbe, Locke struggled to come to terms with the realities of the new world. In that publication, he thought it impractical for government to "suffer one another to go to heaven each one his own way," when, as he believed the revolution had demonstrated, "people . . . are ready to conclude God dishonoured upon every small deviation from that way of his worship which either education or interest hath made sacred to them, and that therefore they ought to vindicate the cause of God with swords in their hands."[12] By the mid-1660s, Locke was reverting to his earlier confidence in toleration, describing to a correspondent in December 1665 how the religiously diverse inhabitants of the German Duchy of Cleves "quietly permit one another to choose their way to heaven," a policy he thought might rather improve the lot of dissenters in Charles II's England.[13] Owen agreed. Throughout the late 1660s, his work on religious toleration and the kind of society that it should uphold would

---

10. Quoted in Roger Woolhouse, *Locke: A Biography* (Cambridge: Cambridge University Press, 2007), 31.

11. "Letter to S. H. [Henry Stubbe] (mid-September? 1659)," in John Locke, *Political Writings*, ed. David Wootton (London: Penguin, 1993), 137.

12. John Locke, *First Tract on Government* (1660), in *Political Writings*, 145.

13. John Locke, "Letter to the Hon. Robert Boyle (12/22 December 1665)," in *Political Writings*, 184. See also Luisa Simonutti, "Political Society and Religious Liberty: Locke at Cleves and in Holland," *British Journal for the History of Philosophy* 14, no. 3 (2006): 413–36.

define arguments and conclusions that would circulate widely in what was coming to be identified as a Whig literary culture—a literary culture of dissenting Protestants who hoped to survive and eventually to build and protect the kind of world in which the spiritual lives of believers might flourish, to the benefit of all.

After the Restoration, Owen's ministry took place among rather ordinary congregants. Now removed from the centers of political power and university administration, Owen had to pay attention for the first time to the mundane realities of economic life, to envisage Christian faithfulness in the everyday world of work, coming to terms with a modest, if often dangerous, middle age. In *A Peace-Offering, or an Apology and Humble Plea for Indulgence and Liberty of Conscience* (1667), Owen recognized that dissenters were "mostly of that sort and condition of men . . . upon whose industry and endeavours, in their several ways and callings, the trade and wealth of the nation do much depend."[14] But he also recognized that some of his fellow dissenters had lost their "trade and wealth," while that of others was being threatened through the system of espionage that rewarded government informants with the property of those whose illegal religious practice they had informed on. As spies stood to gain from the wealth of those they denounced, government policy encouraged the circulation of lies. Quite reasonably, Owen worried about the spread of fake news, which he described in terms that alluded to the exhumation of the corpses of his friends and the revenge that had been taken on the decaying remains of individuals such as Oliver Cromwell. "Stories are told of things past and gone," he reported. "Scattered interest, dissolved intrigues, buried miscarriages, such as never can have any aspect on the present posture of affairs and minds of men in this nation, are gathered together and raked out of their

14. Owen, *Works*, 13:571.

graves," to create "mormoes [monsters] for the affrightment of men from . . . the ways of peace and moderation."[15] Unfounded rumors circulated, associating dissenters with seditious political activities. Owen found these conspiracy theories extremely hard to refute: "If men will take to themselves the liberty of entertaining evil and groundless surmises, it is impossible for us or any living to set bounds to their imaginations."[16] Believers had to find a way to live alongside those who were prepared to believe the worst of them. And so, in the late 1660s, as dangers of the Clarendon Code began to mitigate, Owen turned his attention to the place of Protestant dissenters in English public life and the public good of true spirituality.

Owen grounded his political theory in ideas about citizenship. In an anonymous tract published in 1667, he argued that "every Englishman" was born with an interest in the nation, "in the policy, government, and laws thereof, with the benefits and advantages of them, and the obedience that is due unto them."[17] He explained that Protestant dissenters were willing to accept their obligations as citizens, but because of their conscientious objection to Anglican worship, they found themselves subject to "ecclesiastical censures," as well as to "outward, pecuniary, and corporal punishments," including being deprived of "liberty, freedom, and benefit of the laws of the land"—and sometimes of life itself. On this basis, "great multitudes" had been excommunicated for not attending Anglican worship and had been "cast . . . into the condition of men outlawed and deprived of all privileges of their birthright as Englishmen." Others, like John Bunyan, whom Owen would later befriend, had been "cast into prisons, where they lie perishing (sundry being dead in that state already), whilst

---

15. Owen, *Works*, 13:521.
16. Owen, *Works*, 13:547.
17. Owen, *Works*, 13:531–32.

their families are starved or reduced to the utmost extremity of poverty for want of those supplies which their industry formerly furnished them withal." This policy achieved nothing of value to the state, for "hands . . . by this means are taken off from labour, . . . stocks from employment, . . . minds from contrivances of industry," while "poverty . . . is brought on families"—all to the detriment of the "common good."[18] Meanwhile, those responsible for this persecution seemed to believe that "they alone were to be esteemed Englishmen, and that not only as unto all privileges and advantages attending that title, but so far, also, as to desire that all who differ from them should be exterminated from their native soil."[19] Owen believed that there was no justification for this action. Dissenters were not revolutionaries. "Magistracy we own as the ordinance of God," he explained, and "nonconformity" to the established church did not represent any dangerous "dissent" from its doctrine. But government believed the worst of the nonconformists, who were facing the "forfeiture of all their public rights as Englishmen, and benefit of their private estates."[20] Like Locke, Owen emphasized how English law contrasted in this regard with that of other European powers, including Poland and France, where the conscientious rights of religious dissenters were better respected. The disastrous effect of making church and state coterminous was to infringe on the birthrights of some of those Englishmen who cared most about the good of church and state.

Owen's political enthusiasms cooled in middle age. By the late 1660s, his attitude to the "powers that be" was quite different from the revolutionary ideas he had entertained as a younger man. In the late 1640s, he had argued that the English Civil Wars

---

18. Owen, *Works*, 13:523.
19. Owen, *Works*, 13:520.
20. Owen, *Works*, 13:548, 552–53.

were motivated by religious concerns and that the cause of true religion depended on military conquest, but now he was arguing the opposite case.[21] Thankful for the king's indemnity in the Act of Oblivion (1660), Owen insisted that the new community of Protestant dissenters had "no form of government, civil or ecclesiastical, to impose on the nation," that they laid "no pretence unto power to be exercised on the persons of any of his majesty's subjects," and that they had "no expectations from persons or nations, that might induce us to further or promote any sinister aims of other men." Nonconformists "covet no men's silver or gold, their places or preferments," he explained. "The utmost of our aim is to pass the residue of our pilgrimage in peace, serving God in the way of our devotion." True spirituality was politically passive, he now believed. And, he insisted, submission to government would remain, even if persecution continued. If liberty be denied, "and we must yet be scattered over the face of the earth, we shall yet pray for the prosperity of his majesty and the land of our nativity, patiently bearing the indignation of the Lord, against whom we have sinned, and waiting for his salvation."[22] For Owen, even in such difficult circumstances, the spiritual life was a quiet life: "They are no great things which we desire for ourselves, the utmost of our aim being to pass the remainder of the few days of our pilgrimage in the land of our nativity, serving the Lord according to what he hath been pleased to reveal of his mind and will unto us."[23]

Owen's political theory—undeveloped as it was—made a very significant contribution to the emergence of the political tradition that has since been described as classical liberalism.

21. Owen, *Works*, 13:548; Crawford Gribben, *John Owen and English Puritanism: Experiences of Defeat*, Oxford Studies in Historical Theology (Oxford: Oxford University Press, 2016), 53.

22. Owen, *Works*, 13:549.

23. Owen, *Works*, 13:555.

His work anticipated by a few decades Locke's *Two Treatises of Government* (1689), which would make the best-known intervention in this emerging defense of civil and political liberty. The younger man would certainly have concurred with his former college dean that the "great fundamental law amongst men, from which all others spring, and whereby they ought to be regulated, is that law of nature by which they are disposed unto civil society, for the good of the whole and every individual thereof." Both men would have agreed that this "law of nature" did not require uniformity of mind any more than any other kind of uniformity, whether of "stature and form of visage, or . . . the same measure of intellectual abilities, or the same conception of all objects of a rational understanding."[24] Locke and Owen both thought it impossible that "all men may be of one mind in the matter of the worship of God."[25] And both would have insisted that "one principle of the law of nature, to which we owe the benefits of human conversation and administration of justice," is that "those differences amongst men which unto them are absolutely unavoidable, and therefore in themselves not intrenching upon nor disannulling the good of the whole . . . should be foreborne and allowed among them." These differences should be tolerated because any "endeavour for their extinguishment must irresistibly extinguish the community itself" and because the "harmony" that "riseth from such differences" represents the "chiefest glory and beauty of civil society."[26] Society could not command the mental life of its citizens, for the "empire of conscience belonged unto God alone," Owen explained.[27] But the toleration in civil society of these kinds of competing claims of conscience showed the

---

24. Owen, *Works*, 13:556.
25. Owen, *Works*, 13:567–68.
26. Owen, *Works*, 13:556–57.
27. Owen, *Works*, 13:565.

"glory," "beauty," and "harmony" that the "law of nature" enabled.

This emphasis on the "law of nature" shows how, by the late 1660s, Owen had moved from a Constantinian to a Lutheran view of church-state relations, in which the church was governed by Scripture, while civil society operated on other principles.[28] Owen underscored this argument in the method as well as the conclusions of his argument. His case depended on logic and classical citation; while he made general points about religion and its public performance, his political writings did not advance on the basis of biblical exposition. This marked a major change from his work in the late 1640s and early 1650s. His preaching in that earlier period did not hesitate to fashion English politics on the basis of Old Testament precedents. But in the 1660s, Owen was more interested in drawing lessons for English politics from the "law of nature" and the life of Jesus.

The movement from Old to New Testament precedents is a striking difference in Owen's political writing. Jesus reproved the "sins of men . . . with all authority," but with the "persons of men," Jesus was "always meek and tender, as coming to save, and not to destroy." "In the things of man," Owen explained, "he referred all unto the just authority and righteous laws of men; but in the things of God never gave the least intimation of severity, but only in his holy threats of future evil in the world to come, upon men's final impenitency and unbelief."[29] Owen saw no place for force to be used in imposing religious uniformity: "It must needs seem strange that men can persuade themselves that they do that for Christ which they cannot once think or imagine that he would do himself." Anyone who had "read the

28. David VanDrunen, *Natural Law and the Two Kingdoms: A Study in the Development of Reformed Social Thought*, Emory University Studies in Law and Religion (Grand Rapids, MI: Eerdmans, 2009), 152–72.

29. Owen, *Works*, 13:559.

gospel . . . is a competent judge whether external force in these things do more answer the spirit of Christ or that from which he suffered."[30] For Owen, the "spirit of Christ" could not support sedition, though he might have been exaggerating when he claimed that nonconformists, more than any other party, were committed to "cordial adherence unto and defence of public peace and tranquillity."[31] The responsibility of believers was to "live peacefully in subjection to the government of the nation, and usefully amongst their neighbours," encouraging "the mutual trust, confidence, and assurance between all sorts of persons, which is the abiding foundation of public peace and prosperity."[32] The only permissible resistance to government was passive:

> Although we are persuaded that what we profess and practise is according unto the mind of Christ, yet because it is our lot and portion to have our governors and rulers otherwise minded, we are contented to be dealt withal so as the blessed gospel will warrant any to deal with them who are so far in the wrong as we are supposed to be. And if herein we cannot prevail, we shall labour to possess our souls in patience, and to commit our cause to Him that judgeth righteously.[33]

In that confidence, "whatever is ours, whatever is in our power, whatever God hath intrusted us with the disposal of, we willingly resign and give up to the will and commands of our superiors; but as to our minds and consciences in the things of his worship and service, he hath reserved the sovereignty of them unto himself."[34] True spirituality could have significant political costs.

---

30. Owen, *Works*, 13:560.
31. Owen, *Works*, 13:570.
32. Owen, *Works*, 13:572–73.
33. Owen, *Works*, 13:562.
34. Owen, *Works*, 13:574.

Of course, as with his former student Locke, Owen's commitment to "liberty of conscience" was never absolute.[35] He made no argument that Catholics or adherents of religions that did not worship "the God of Israel" should be tolerated.[36] In this, he may not have appreciated that the claims he made on behalf of Protestant dissenters might apply with equal weight to other proscribed religious communities: it was not only Protestant dissenters that had, "by the fears, dangers, and sufferings which they have passed through, evidenced to all the world that the liberty and freedom of their consciences is of more consideration with them than all other things whatever."[37] Perhaps he simply didn't have enough leisure to see this parallel. His views were vigorously attacked by Richard Perrinchief, in *Indulgence Not Justified* (1668), and became the focus of protracted debate.[38] Owen worried about the effects on the godly of political debate: "I fear whilst men are so engaged in their thoughts about what is good and convenient for them at the present, they do scarce sufficiently ponder what account of their actions they must make hereafter."[39] Theorizing about the good life could become an end in itself, he advised his readers: "Take care that we add not unto the evils of the days wherein we live."[40]

Church Life

Owen's theological convictions were unmodified by the changing political circumstances of the later 1660s.[41] In his occasional

35. Owen, *Works*, 13:528.
36. Owen, *Works*, 13:562, 569.
37. Owen, *Works*, 13:536.
38. For an account of this controversy, see John Locke, *An Essay concerning Toleration, and Other Writings on Law and Politics, 1667–1683*, ed. J. R. Milton and Philip Milton, in *The Clarendon Edition of the Works of John Locke*, ed. M. A. Stewart, Peter Nidditch, and John Yolton (Oxford: Clarendon, 2006), 11–26, 152–57.
39. Owen, *Works*, 13:522.
40. Owen, *Works*, 13:543.
41. Owen, *Works*, 13:551.

writings on political themes, Owen continued to point his critics to the confession of faith that the Congregational churches had agreed on in 1658, complaining that those who attacked the Savoy Declaration had not taken the trouble to read it, despite the fact that it had been widely circulated and (though the evidence for this claim is not now clear) translated into "sundry other languages."[42] Owen argued that confessions of faith were necessary to set forth the faith of associated congregations.[43] His confessional commitments continued, but since the late 1650s, his commitment to church life had, if anything, intensified, as an essential context for the pursuit of the spiritual life.

Owen's fullest discussion of congregational life appeared in 1667. *A Brief Instruction in the Worship of God*, which he published anonymously, provided an extended catechetical defense of what would become known as the regulative principle of worship. In this widely circulated book, which rapidly passed through a second edition, Owen argued that "God is to be worshipped . . . according to his own will and appointment" and that the content of this worship was to be "drawn from the Scriptures alone."[44] His rhetoric associated the worship of the Roman Catholic Church with that of the Church of England, the congregations of which were now often returning to the elaborate liturgical structures of the Laudian devotion that had caused so much controversy before the English Civil Wars.[45] He contrasted the simplicity of New Testament principles with the flourish and ostentation of those who had "changed the whole spiritual worship of the church into a theatrical, pompous show of carnal devotion."[46] Owen emphasized that his

42. Owen, *Works*, 13:546, 577.
43. Owen, *Works*, 15:530.
44. Owen, *Works*, 15:448, 450.
45. See John Spurr, *The Restoration Church of England, 1646–1689* (New Haven, CT: Yale University Press, 1991).
46. Owen, *Works*, 15:468.

criticism was not directed against the Church of England as such: in *The Grounds and Reasons on Which Protestant Dissenters Desire Their Liberty* (which Owen's nineteenth-century editor attributes to him and dates to sometime shortly after 1667), he suggested that in exchange for toleration, dissenting ministers could sign the Thirty-Nine Articles as evidence of their fidelity to the constitutional settlement.[47] After all, he claimed, other than in its discussion of church government, the Savoy Declaration might have expanded on, but it never contradicted, the Anglican articles. Owen, therefore, had "no new faith to declare, no new doctrine to teach, no private opinions to divulge, no point or truth do we profess, no not one, which hath not been declared, taught, divulged, and esteemed as the common doctrine of the church of England, ever since the Reformation."[48] Owen recognized the existence of confessional variety within the Reformed tradition but insisted that the Savoy Declaration did not

> disturb the harmony that is in the confessions of the reformed churches, being in all material points the same with them, and no otherwise differing from any of them in things of less importance than as they do from one another, and as all confessions have done, since the first introduction of their use into the churches of God.[49]

There were only minor differences between the Anglican and Congregational confessions, he believed, and those differences hardly represented a threat to the state.

Owen's target was the style of worship that paid no attention to the requirements or silences of the New Testament and that bore witness to the preferences of the worshiper

---

47. Owen, *Works*, 13:578.
48. Owen, *Works*, 13:552.
49. Owen, *Works*, 13:551.

rather than the one who was being worshiped. The issue was more than a matter of expressing a preference when presented with a menu of devotional options. He understood the situation in apocalyptic terms: he believed that the "false worship" that represented a "departure from the institutions of Christ" constituted the "great apostasy of the church in the last days, foretold in the Scripture, and which God threateneth to punish and revenge," and he argued that this worship was, in fact, the "cause of all the plagues and destructions" that were being poured out on England "by the righteous judgement of God."[50] Recent disasters were evidence that something was going seriously wrong, and Owen traced the problem to its root: the Great Plague (1665–1666) and the Great Fire of London (1666) had been provoked by flamboyant ritualism in English parish churches.

In contrast with Anglican apostasy, Owen emphasized the simplicity, privacy, and even secrecy of the kind of worship that had been commanded in the New Testament. He believed that a great deal of activity in worship would go unnoticed by the world. "Some duties of obedience there are which the world neither doth nor can discern in believers," he explained; "such are their faith, inward holiness, purity of heart, heavenly-mindedness, sincere mortification of indwelling sin." He argued that other kinds of activity in worship "ought to be hid" from the world, such as "personal prayer and alms." But while many of the activities of individuals would go unnoticed by the world, the worship of churches could not be concealed, for the activity of congregations was "that which the world may see and take notice of, and that which, unless in case of persecution, ought not to be hid from them." A "happy and a blessed thing it is to suffer for the observation of the special commands of Christ,"

---

50. Owen, *Works*, 15:476–77.

and the responsibility for public worship remained even when times were unpropitious.[51]

For Owen, the worship outlined in the New Testament was especially linked to creation and the new covenant. He argued that worship was "natural," in a choice of vocabulary that would resonate in his political writing, and that an appropriate response to general revelation would recognize God as "sovereign Lord, First Cause, Last End, Judge, and Rewarder of all men." The responsibility for worship was built into the "nature of man, as that which suited, directed, and enabled him to answer the law of his creation."[52] Idolatry, by contrast, fought against the "light of nature and principles of reason."[53] For Owen, the principles that govern the church were not different in kind from the principles that should govern the state. Nevertheless, he insisted, only those who could make a convincing claim to be a member of the new covenant, through a narrative of conversion, should be allowed to become members of a local church.[54] He dealt sensitively with the worries of those who could not date their conversion, and in his *Discourse concerning Christian Love and Peace* (1672), he explained that individuals could become members of local churches if they could evidence "baptism, with a voluntary credible profession of faith, repentance, and obedience unto the Lord Christ, in his commands and institutions," while making a "personal avowment of that faith whereinto they were baptised."[55] The emphasis on individual faith was essential because Owen understood the local congregation as an expression of the body of Christ, with its members uniting together on the basis that they were already united to

---

51. Owen, *Works*, 15:474.
52. Owen, *Works*, 15:447.
53. Owen, *Works*, 15:449.
54. Owen, *Works*, 15:526–27.
55. Owen, *Works*, 6:599; 15:95, 154.

him. From this theological claim Owen outlined guidelines for congregational participation that focused on prayer, preaching, the singing of psalms, governance by elders, an appropriate use of discipline, and regular participation in the sacraments. Our "implanting into Christ is represented and signified by our baptism," he argued, "as also our communion with him in his death, by the supper of the Lord."[56] And so, following Calvin's dictum that word and sacrament should never be separated, he argued that the Congregational churches should share together in the Lord's Supper on a weekly basis, as the visual reminder of their being held together in the new covenant.[57] These ideas percolated throughout *A Brief Instruction in the Worship of God.*

But it is not clear whether Owen was able to implement each of these principles within his own congregation. In the late 1660s, his church comprised around thirty members, many of them from one extended family and its network of friends. Several members of his fellowship kept detailed notes of its worship, which, taken together, provide an insightful if not entirely well-rounded account of the life of this small congregation.[58] In 1673, which turned out to be one of the most eventful years in the life of the church, Sir John Hartopp and Lucy Hutchinson, a regular attender who was not a member, took notes of Owen's preaching on around twenty-one different occasions. Their notes record the life of a busy church in a dangerous situation.

The circumstances among Congregational churches more broadly was discouraging. Hutchinson recorded Owen's observation that "churches . . . that were strict and close in their walking with God are growne more remisse & coole in their zeale

---

56. Owen, *Works*, 15:473.

57. Owen, *Works*, 15:512.

58. *The Works of Lucy Hutchinson*, ed. Elizabeth Clarke, David Norbrook, and Jane Stevenson, with textual introductions by Jonathan Gibson and editorial assistance from Mark Burden and Alice Eardley (Oxford: Oxford University Press, 2018), 2:28. An additional 1673 sermon may be found in Owen, *Works*, 16:530.

. . . by conformities falling off from their first love."[59] And the political situation remained dangerously unpredictable. In March 1672, Charles II had issued his Declaration of Indulgence, which suspended the penal laws against Catholics and Protestant dissenters and offered these communities greater freedom for public meetings and even the prospect of religious liberty. This gesture appalled members of the Cavalier Parliament, which in February 1673 passed a Test Act requiring the occupants of civil and military offices to subscribe to the oaths of supremacy and allegiance, to affirm a statement rejecting the Roman Catholic doctrine of transubstantiation, and to take Communion in an Anglican parish church.

The Test Act reintroduced the specter of religious persecution and outed the king's brother, the Duke of York and future King James II, as a convert to Catholicism, but it is not clear what consequences it had for the members of Owen's church, nor how it affected their weekly routine of meetings. But "routine" may be too strong a term to describe the church's life in this difficult year. While most of the meetings on which notes were taken occurred on weekdays, there does not appear to be any pattern in the days on which the church met: Owen preached on every day of the week at some point during the year, perhaps following the practice of other dissenting churches in the period, as a way to make life a little more difficult for government informants.[60] It was one thing for Owen to idealize church order in *A Brief Instruction in the Worship of God*, but it was quite another to work out those principles in a situation in which so much was constantly at risk.

In such troubled times, leadership was key to the security of the Congregational churches. The church's year began with the ordination of an elder, on Thursday, January 23, 1673,

59. Notebook of Lucy Hutchinson, DD/HU3, 229, Inspire Nottinghamshire Archives.
60. *Works of Lucy Hutchinson*, 2:28.

when Owen preached on Ephesians 4:8, referring to the Geneva Bible's translation of Acts 14:23 to defend his claim that elders were appointed by a congregational vote. Having established this point, Owen called on the congregation to assent to the appointment of their new elder by raising their hands.[61] As this event suggests, Owen's laments about the decline of the revolutionary generation—the increasing number of deaths of the preachers who had led the Puritan movement in happier days—was balanced by the appointment of new elders and ministers throughout the dark days of the 1670s and early 1680s. Even as the political climate grew less favorable to dissenting churches, younger men were still prepared to identify with them. This may explain why Owen's preaching throughout this period majored on the theme of endurance. He preached regularly on Hebrews 12:14 in weekday services from November 1671 until August 1673.[62] This concentration of effort in the pulpit contrasts with the rather brief discussion of the verse in the massive commentary on Hebrews that Owen was preparing during this period.[63] But this discussion was immediately relevant to the context of the listeners. If Hebrews as a whole encouraged the "profession of the gospel, under sufferings and afflictions," this verse required that those who were the victims of suffering and affliction should nevertheless "follow peace" with "our enemies . . . our persecutors."[64]

Christians also had to "follow peace" with fellow believers—a point that Owen emphasized in his preaching over the

---

61. Owen, *Works*, 9:438.

62. Notebook of Sir John Hartopp, Dr. Williams's Library (DWL), and Sermons by Dr. Owen, Mr. Perrott, and Others, 1672–1675, British Library (BL): Tuesday, February 11, 1672/73, DWL NCL/L6/2 and BL Sloane 3680; Thursday, February 24, 1672/73, DWL NCL/L6/2 and BL Sloane 3680; Tuesday, May 13, 1673, DWL NCL/L6/2; Tuesday, May 27, 1673, DWL NCL/L6/2; Tuesday, July 29, 1673, DWL NCL/L6/2; Tuesday, August 12, 1673, DWL NCL/L6/2 and BL Sloane 3680. See also the sermons transcribed in Owen, *Works*, vol. 9.

63. Owen, *Works*, 24:284–88.

64. Owen, *Works*, 24:286.

summer, when his small congregation of around 30 individuals, many with high social standing and close connection to the old republic, merged with the more socially diverse congregation of 136 individuals that had been led by Joseph Caryl before his recent death.[65] The two congregations met for the first time, on the Leadenhall Street premises that belonged to Caryl's group, on Thursday, June 5, when Owen marked their merger with a sermon on love.[66] Owen had to warn those members who had enjoyed "providential advantages" in "birth, education, inheritance, estate, titles, places" not to remain distant from the "meanest, the poorest saint that belongs unto the congregation."[67] His choice of text allowed him to point his listeners toward their responsibilities to each other, turning their attention away from the well-known ministers who had led them. "Churches have been apt to place their communion too much, if not solely, in the participation of the same ordinances, depending upon the same pastor and teacher," he explained. Owen worried about the culture of celebrity within the dissenting churches and warned the combined congregation that this dependence on high-profile preachers "may be without any real communion" between those who listened to them.[68] What mattered, he emphasized, was not so much the gift of the preacher as the extent to which church members demonstrated their gifts toward each other. After all, Owen continued, a "church full of love, is a church well built up. I had rather see a church filled with love a thousand times, than filled with the best, the brightest, and most glorious gifts and parts that any men in this world may be partakers of."[69]

---

65. The membership lists in 1673 of the Owen and Caryl congregations may be found in T. G. Crippen, "Dr. Watts's Church Book," *Transactions of the Congregational Historical Society* 1 (1901–1904): 27.

66. Owen, *Works*, 9:256–57.

67. Owen, *Works*, 9:270.

68. Owen, *Works*, 9:266.

69. Owen, *Works*, 9:268.

And so, three days later, on Sunday, June 8, when the combined congregation celebrated its first Communion service, Owen's mind was still very much focused on how believers should relate to one another: "The Lord lift us up above our fears, and give us a view by faith . . . that he personally loved us, even this whole church."[70] For, as he put it in a sermon on June 20, believers facing "temporall evils" may experience the consolation of communion with God, the sustaining power of spiritual life.[71]

Despite Owen's preference for weekly Communion, his new church seemed to be settling into a monthly celebration of the Supper. They communed again on Sunday, July 6, and met on the following day to listen to another sermon.[72] At the Table, Owen took care to distinguish the Supper from the preaching of the gospel. In the gospel, he argued, "the person of the Father is particularly looked on as proposing and tendering Christ to us." In the Supper, by contrast, "Christ makes an immediate tender of himself, and calls our faith to have respect to his grace, to his love, and to his readiness to unite and spiritually incorporate with us."[73] Owen followed this short address at the Table with a more extended discussion on the following day. Preaching on the phrase "Take, eat" (1 Cor. 11:24), he explained "what it is to obtain a sacramental part of Jesus Christ in this ordinance of the Lord's Supper."[74] This sermon was strikingly similar to the previous day's address at the Table. Now expanded in length and thematic range, Owen's appeal for individual reception of Christ at the Table was paralleled with his appeal that those who sit at the Table should also accept one another. To sit at the Lord's Table was to "sit down . . . as

---

70. Owen, *Works*, 16:527 [the original Goold edition places this at 17:595].
71. Notebook of Lucy Hutchinson, DD/HU3, 210, Inspire Nottinghamshire Archives.
72. Owen, *Works*, 9:563–66; 16:528–30.
73. Owen, *Works*, 16:529.
74. Owen, *Works*, 9:563.

those that are the Lord's friends."[75] And, he might have added, the consequence of being accepted by God in the gospel is that we extend the same hospitality to those with whom he has put us in gospel fellowship.

There is certainly evidence that Owen's listeners understood the importance of being together. Several new members were added in 1673, including the auspiciously named Cromwell Fleetwood.[76] Others wished they could attend the congregation but found that circumstances prevented it: Lewis Du Moulin, a former Oxford academic, admitted that he liked "the congregation of Dr. Owen . . . best," but being "old and sickly," he found that Leadenhall Street was too "far distant" for frequent travel.[77] Others attended without becoming members. During the spring and summer months, Lucy Hutchinson, widow and memoirist of the famous Civil War officer Colonel John Hutchinson, took notes on several of Owen's sermons, while also around this time beginning a project to translate into English the early sections of his most formidable theological work, *Theologoumena Pantodapa* (1661). Others attended the congregation on a more casual basis. Ralph Thorseby was typical of many churchgoers, whose habits of "sermon gadding" stretched across the division between Anglicans and dissenters in Restoration London. Thorseby attended the sermons of a wide range of preachers to take notes that he and his friends would share in the "Tuesday-night meeting at our house," in which attendees "repeated" the sermons they had heard as a collective devotional activity.[78] In September 1677, he listened

---

75. Owen, *Works*, 9:566.
76. Crippen, "Dr. Watts's Church Book," 27.
77. Geoffrey F. Nuttall, "Milton's Churchmanship in 1659: His Letter to Jean de Labadie," *Milton Quarterly* 35, no. 4 (2001): 229, citing F. J. Powicke, "Dr. Lewis Du Moulin's Vindication of the Congregational Way," *Congregational Historical Society Transactions* 9 (1924–1926): 219–36, at 234–35.
78. *The Diary of Ralph Thorseby, F.R.S.*, ed. Joseph Hunter (London, 1830), 1:6.

to Owen, who "preached very well of the power of Christ; but was sore thronged, that I could neither write nor hear very well."[79] He was frustrated on his next attempt to listen to Owen, just a few days later, when he was distracted by "many thoughts and imaginations" and left the service to go shopping for the colored crayons he needed to pursue his new interest in art.[80] Owen recognized how much dissenters could contribute to England's growing economy—and how the new culture of commodity could threaten a serious commitment to the pursuit of spiritual life.

Conclusion

Owen well understood the challenges of middle life. In spring 1660, in his mid-forties, he faced a horrific crisis. It was not simply personal or political, though the achievements of his career had been invalidated by England's second revolution inside fifteen years. It was also a theological crisis: his understanding of providence was shattered. He rapidly retreated from the prophetic and political panorama that he had outlined in his sermons to Parliament in the 1640s and 1650s. In the 1660s, as he slowly reemerged into public view, he appeared most concerned to speak of the duty of dissenters to be good neighbors, to make effective social and economic contributions, and, above all, to live quietly and mind their own business (1 Thess. 4:11; 2 Thess. 3:12; 1 Tim. 2:2). The spiritual life was a quiet life, a life that made positive contributions where it could but always looked beyond its achievements in this world. And this is how Owen was remembered by two of the leading figures of the American Revolution. On October 6, 1800, Benjamin Rush wrote to Thomas Jefferson to remind him of how radically John

---

79. *Diary of Ralph Thorseby*, 1:4.
80. *Diary of Ralph Thorseby*, 1:5.

Owen, a "sincere friend to liberty," had moved away from his early political concerns: "He has left many Volumes of Sermons behind him, that are so wholly religious, that no One from reading them, could tell, in what country, or age they were preached."[81] In the experience of defeat, Owen had come to contrast the difficulties of the Restoration with glory in another world: "It is but yet a little while before it will be no grief of heart unto us for to have done or suffered any thing for the name of the Lord Jesus."[82] In the meantime, believers were to do what they could to contribute to the good of their society, in the fellowship of the church, while always remembering that there was much more to spiritual life than the temporal achievements of a dangerous middle age.

---

81. "To Thomas Jefferson from Benjamin Rush, 6 October 1800," in *The Papers of Thomas Jefferson*, vol. 32, *1 June 1800 to 16 February 1801*, ed. Barbara B. Oberg (Princeton, NJ: Princeton University Press, 2005), 204–7.

82. Owen, *Works*, 13:543.

4

Death and Eternal Life

"Some say God kist his soule out," Owen observed of the death of Moses, in a sermon that Lucy Hutchinson recorded in April 1673. While the patriarch had walked with God throughout his adult life and carried responsibility for civil leadership, the "neer communion" with God that he enjoyed in his final days had turned the experience of death into an unexpected blessing.[1] Of course, Owen recognized, death would always be an enemy, but believers could face its terrors with confidence. For the Christian, in the new covenant, death represented a late stage of progressive sanctification, the continuing increase in holiness that was the fruit of God's work in the life of the believer. Death was not the end but another step on the journey toward the consummation of spiritual life.

Owen expected that Christians would face death with apprehension, but he wanted to encourage his readers with the thought of what lay beyond. He expected that Christians would find the intermediate state, with the soul living apart from the

---

1. Notebook of Lucy Hutchinson, DD/HU3, 199, Inspire Nottinghamshire Archives.

body, to be an unfamiliar mode of existence: in heaven, the soul would be operating without the sense perceptions that it had known during the time of its attachment to flesh, blood, and bone, in a manner analogous in earthly life only to dreaming in time of sleep. But Christians were not to anticipate that this experience of being disembodied would somehow be permanent or that they would have to get used to a new kind of life without a body. Human beings are souls with bodies, Owen insisted, and their salvation had implications for both. The purposes of saving grace would be realized only when the body was resurrected and the believer was glorified to be fully like Christ. This last stage of salvation, and the only stage of grace that would be enjoyed simultaneously by all the elect, would be brought to its harmonious completion at the second coming. And it would offer new prospects for worship. In a significant revision of Thomistic tradition, Owen insisted that glorified saints would apprehend the "glory of God in the face of Jesus Christ" (2 Cor. 4:6). The beatific vision would be finally and fully realized not in a sight of the divine essence, as Thomas Aquinas had argued, but in that of the glorified humanity of Jesus Christ.[2] In later life, Owen became increasingly aware of his mortality: "I know not how others bear up their hearts and spirits," he confessed. "For my part, I have much ado to keep from continual longing after the embraces of the dust and shades of the grave, as a curtain drawn over the rest in

---

2. Owen's contribution to the discussion about the object of the beatific vision is the subject of some debate: Suzanne McDonald, "Beholding the Glory of God in the Face of Jesus Christ: John Owen and the 'Reforming' of the Beatific Vision," in *The Ashgate Research Companion to John Owen's Theology*, ed. Kelly M. Kapic and Mark Jones (Aldershot, UK: Ashgate, 2012), 141–58; Simon Francis Gaine, "Thomas Aquinas and John Owen on the Beatific Vision: A Reply to Suzanne McDonald," *New Blackfriars* 97 (2016): 432–46; Hans Boersma, "Thomas Aquinas on the Beatific Vision: A Christological Deficit," *TheoLogica: An International Journal for Philosophy of Religion and Philosophical Theology* 2, no. 2 (2018), accessed April 23, 2019, https://ojs.uclouvain .be/index.php/theologica/article/view/14733; Boersma, *Seeing God: The Beatific Vision in Christian Tradition* (Grand Rapids, MI: Eerdmans, 2018), 321–27.

another world."[3] Nevertheless, "our eyes were made to see our redeemer," Owen insisted, in his *Meditations and Discourses on the Glory of Christ* (1684), the book that he proofread on his deathbed as he looked forward to his first physical view of his Savior.[4] For Christians, the resurrection and glorification of the body brought spiritual life to its happiest completion, in the eternal vision of God in Christ.

Owen and Eschatology

Owen's almost rhapsodic account of the beatific vision was the logical conclusion to his long preoccupation with personal and cosmic eschatology. From the earliest days of his ministry, he had been living with the end in view. He began his writing career in "these last evil days of the world," and that vision of the end directed the purpose of his life, as if the end of spiritual living determined the means by which that life should be pursued.[5] Owen drew on his eschatology to explain the political and cultural changes through which he lived—from civil war, regicide, and republic to Restoration, the Great Fire of London, and the devastation of the plague—and to understand, and later rethink, how he should relate to them. Throughout his life, Owen's interest in eschatology was reflected in his confidence about the globalization of Protestant Christianity, as well as in his worries about the immediate prospects of English Protestantism. That interest became personally relevant through his experience of bereavement and, ultimately, as he faced the prospect of his own death. In this enduring interest, Owen resembled many other Puritans, for whom personal and cosmic eschatology were standard theological themes. But this interest in eschatology also distinguished Owen from many of

3. Owen, *Works*, 21:512, commenting on Heb. 5:7.
4. Owen, *Works*, 1:412.
5. Owen, *Works*, 8:191.

his contemporaries: his lifelong study of individual and cosmic ends drove his convictions about spiritual life, even as it displayed some significant changes of theological opinion and his increasing variance from Western catholic thought.

Owen's earliest writing indicates his interest in "knowing the times." *The Duty of Pastors and People Distinguished* (1644) reflected his sense that the "glass of our lives seems to run and keep pace with the extremity of time. The end of those 'ends of the world' which began with the gospel is doubtless coming upon us. . . . Christ shakes the glass, many minutes of that hour cannot remain."[6] Two years into the First Civil War, and after a generation of sectarian warfare on the continent, Owen was sure that its political turmoil, massive casualties, and administrative chaos should be explained in terms of an impending apocalypse.[7] And he made this explicit while preaching to members of Parliament (MPs) on January 30, 1649, the day after the execution of Charles I, when he described those responsible for the regicide as men who had been "called . . . forth" at the beginning of God's "rolling up of the nation's heavens like a scroll, to serve him in your generation in the high places of Armageddon."[8]

Owen was rarely so incautious or eschatologically committed. He understood that his prophetic hope was inevitably political, in that the globalization of the gospel that he expected would require radical changes in the social, cultural, and public, as well as religious, life of nations: "Most nations in their civil constitution lie out of order for the bringing in of the interest of Christ," he suggested, and so "they must be shaken up and new disposed of, that all obstacles may be taken away."[9] This,

6. Owen, *Works*, 13:5.
7. See, for example, Peter H. Wilson, *The Thirty Years War: Europe's Tragedy* (Cambridge, MA: Belknap Press of Harvard University Press, 2009).
8. Owen, *Works*, 8:129.
9. Owen, *Works*, 8:321.

he understood, was what was happening in England during the wars of the 1640s: "The Lord Jesus Christ, by his mighty power, in these latter days, as antichristian tyranny draws to its period, will so far shake and translate the political heights, governments, and strength of the nations, as shall serve for the full bringing in of his own peaceable kingdom," until the nations become a "quiet habitation for the people of the Most High."[10] But unlike many of his peers, including some members of the Westminster Assembly, Owen never offered dates for the fulfillment of prophetic events, and he refused to follow many of his contemporaries, especially Congregational ministers, into speculation about the millennium: "For the personal reign of the Lord Jesus on earth, I leave it to them with whose discoveries I am not, and curiosities I would not be, acquainted, Acts iii. 21."[11]

Owen refused to commit himself to any millennial theory. He lamented the "endless and irreconcilable contests" of those who debated

> whether over and beyond all these the Lord Christ shall not bear an outward, visible, glorious rule, setting up a kingdom like those of the world, to be ruled by strength and power; and if so, when or how it shall be brought in,—into whose hands the administration of it shall be committed, and upon what account,—whether he will personally walk therein or no,—whether it shall be clearly distinct from the rule he now bears in the world, or only differenced by more glorious degrees and manifestations of his power. . . . This we find, by woful experience, that all who, from the spirituality of the rule of Christ, and delight therein, have degenerated into carnal apprehensions of the beauty and

---

10. Owen, *Works*, 8:260.
11. Owen, *Works*, 8:259.

glory of it, have, for the most part, been given up to carnal actings, suited to such apprehensions.[12]

He was quite clear that while biblical prophecy could explain the chaos of Western Europe after thirty years of war, it did not provide a warrant for military aggression. And unlike some of his peers, he did not believe that eschatology provided the basis for foreign policy: "I speak not with respect to any engagements of war with foreign nations;—what have I to do with things that are above me?"[13] Consequently, he did not support those who drew on their expectations of a future millennium to justify the "disturbance of all order and authority, civil and spiritual," or to "introduce such confusion and disorder as the soul of the Lord Jesus doth exceedingly abhor."[14] The values of political radicalism were opposed to those of the gospel. In this respect, Owen remained permanently out of step with his closest colleagues in the leadership of the Congregational churches, including Thomas Goodwin, whose distinctive millennial expectations set them apart from their contemporaries in other emerging denominational communities.[15] Owen affirmed the prospect of a latter glory of the church without developing any specific millennial theory to explain it.

If he preferred to remain vague about certain elements of cosmic eschatology, Owen did take pains to relate biblical prophecy to specific instances in history. In his early preaching, in the 1640s, he advanced preterist readings of key passages in Matthew 24 and Revelation 6, which he associated, respectively, with the fall of Jerusalem in AD 70 and the fall of the Roman Empire in the fifth century. In doing so, Owen

---

12. Owen, *Works*, 8:373.
13. Owen, *Works*, 8:322.
14. Owen, *Works*, 8:259.
15. Crawford Gribben, *The Puritan Millennium: Literature and Theology, 1550–1682* (Dublin: Four Courts, 2000), 55.

was drawing on a minority position within the tradition of Reformed interpretation. But he departed from that tradition altogether when he sought references to the English Civil Wars in the closing chapters of Revelation.[16] In this narrative, Owen presented the conflict between king and Parliament as being part of a redemptive purpose in English history, a local example of how "God in his appointed time will bring forth the kingdom of the Lord Christ unto more glory and power than in former days." He believed that the promised "glory and power" would involve the church enjoying "fullness of peace" and "purity and beauty of ordinances and gospel worship," pursuing "the full casting out and rejecting of all will-worship," while receiving "multitudes of converts, many persons," witnessing the "professed subjection of the nations throughout the whole world unto the Lord Christ," and participating in the "most glorious and dreadful breaking of all that rise in opposition to him."[17] In his early career, bursting with eschatological conviction and with confidence about the accuracy of his own interpretation of biblical prophecy, Owen encouraged the MPs who listened to his preaching to

> believe the promises, . . . believe the beast unto destruction, antichrist into the pit, and Magog to ruin. Believe that the enemies of Christ shall be made his footstool, that the nations shall be his inheritance, that he shall reign gloriously in beauty, that he shall smite in pieces the heads over divers nations.[18]

As this statement suggested, Owen's expectation of latter-day glory was inevitably political. The globalization of Protestant Christianity would require the "civil powers of the world,

---

16. Owen, *Works*, 8:321–22.
17. Owen, *Works*, 8:334.
18. Owen, *Works*, 8:335.

after fearful shakings and desolations," to be "disposed of into a useful subserviency to the interest, power, and kingdom of Jesus Christ." Missionary expansion involved constitutional change: "God will shake the heavens and the earth of the nations round about, until all the Babylonish rubbish, all their original engagements to the man of sin, be taken away."[19] And in that constitutional change, the world would be turned upside down. Those who had persecuted believers would be tried by them, "judged and sentenced by the poor creatures whom in this world they continually pursue with all manner of enmity," as the last would finally become the first.[20] Owen based his reading of current affairs on the theory of history that he drew from Scripture.[21] He believed that Daniel had foreseen the "four great empires of the world, which had, and were to have, dominion in and over the places of the church's greatest concernments, and were all to receive their period and destruction by the Lord Christ and his revenging hand."[22] Owen understood that the "fourth beast, without name or special form, is the Roman empire," and he believed that in the tumult of the Thirty Years' War and the English Civil Wars, he was witnessing the final destruction of what had once been the Roman Empire. The fifth kingdom, the kingdom of Christ, would grow in its place, with consequences that Owen could predict.[23] If Owen's reading of prophecy was accurate, and if the events of the English Civil Wars were somehow forecast in Scripture and indicative of the kind of reforms that would accompany the globalization of Protestant Christianity, the execution of Charles I was not likely to remain unique.

---

19. Owen, *Works*, 8:374.
20. Owen, *Works*, 8:372.
21. Owen, *Works*, 8:367.
22. Owen, *Works*, 8:368–69.
23. Owen, *Works*, 8:369.

Nevertheless, even in this early part of his career, Owen's eschatology was not fundamentally a fantasy of revenge, nor entirely focused on the experience of English Protestants. Like many other Puritans, he took an interest in the future of the Jews. Following the interpretive tradition established by the annotations of the Geneva Bible, which was published between 1560 and 1644 and circulated on both sides of the Atlantic in hundreds of thousands of copies, Owen was convinced that the globalization of Protestant Christianity would bring about the latter-day conversion of the Jews. It took some time for Owen to warm to this theme, given the strongly presentist interests of his earliest writings, but by the mid-1650s he had come to insist on the temporal priority of God's work to fulfill his promises to Abraham (as Owen understood them) in bringing his descendants to a recognition that their Messiah was Jesus Christ. He became convinced that Christ would begin his work to advance his kingdom around the world by converting Jews in massive numbers.[24] He came to believe that this claim should be central to the articulation of Christian faith. In 1658, for example, he was part of the committee of Congregational theologians who published the Savoy Declaration, which expected that "in the later days, Antichrist being destroyed, the Jews called, the adversaries of the Kingdom of his dear Son broken, the Churches of Christ being enlarged . . . shall enjoy . . . a more quiet, peaceable and glorious condition."[25] Far from being narrowly focused on his own country or his own religious tradition, Owen expected that the conversion of the Jews to Protestant Christianity would herald a time of blessing for the world.

---

24. Owen, *Works*, 8:375.

25. *A Declaration of the Faith and Order owned and practiced in the Congregational Churches in England; Agreed upon and consented unto by their elders and messengers in their meeting at the Savoy* (London, 1658), 45 (26.5).

Owen did not expect this restoration of the Jews to be merely spiritual. In December 1655, after some very effective petitioning work by Manasseh ben Israel, a Portuguese rabbi who was lobbying English administrators on behalf of his co-religionists, Owen traveled to Whitehall to participate in a meeting with senior government figures, including Oliver Cromwell, to consider whether Jews, who had been expelled from England in 1290, should now be readmitted. The substance of Owen's contribution to this discussion is not now clear, but he did appreciate Manasseh ben Israel's scholarly work, including his translated work *Hope of Israel* (1652), and would most likely have welcomed any opportunity for Jewish people to have improved access to the gospel preaching through which, he expected, they would eventually be persuaded of the claims of Protestant Christianity.

In one statement that reflected an interest that was uncharacteristic of his wider work, Owen suggested that the eventual conversion of the Jews to Protestant Christianity would be accompanied by their return to the promised land. While Jewish people remained scattered among the nations, it was inappropriate, he believed, to "dream of setting up an outward, glorious, visible kingdom of Christ, which he must bear rule in, and over the world." But the end of the Diaspora and the regathering of Jews to the promised land would change everything, and that in favor of English Puritans: "We may lift up our heads toward the fulness of our redemption" when the "seed of Abraham, being multiplied like the stars of heaven and the sands of the sea-shore, shall possess the gates of their enemies, and shall have peace in their borders."[26] He made the point explicitly in his commentary on Hebrews, predicting that Jewish people would experience "restoration unto their own

---

26. Owen, *Works*, 8:376.

land, with a blessed, flourishing, and happy condition therein," a conclusion that he claimed was "acknowledged . . . by all the world that have any acquaintance with these things."[27] Having returned to "their own land," and to faith in the Messiah, the Jews would be "filled . . . with the light and knowledge of the will and worship of God, so as to be a guide and blessing unto the residue of the Gentiles who shall seek after the Lord; and, it may be, be intrusted with great empire and rule in the world."[28]

Owen rarely speculated about the future of the biblical land of Israel, but many of his contemporaries—and at least one of his congregants, Samuel Lee—did not share his hesitation about so doing. Lee had taught at Wadham College, Oxford, in the 1650s, when he may well have known the university's vice-chancellor. Lee's scholarly work crossed several disciplines and demonstrated his eclectic interests. In later life, he repudiated his early enthusiasm for astrology but continued to investigate other fields of what his colleagues would have regarded as speculative knowledge, including biblical prophecy and numerology. In 1677, he published an old manuscript by Giles Fletcher, titled *Israel Redux*, which argued that the ten lost tribes of Israel could be found near the Black Sea. To this work he appended a much longer dissertation of his own, in which he made a case for the "future conversion" of these tribes and their "establishment in their own land," while suggesting various dates in the eighteenth and nineteenth centuries for the fulfillment of these prophetic hopes.[29]

It is telling that Owen did not write in support of Lee's work, despite writing prefaces to books published by other

---

27. Owen, *Works*, 18:434 [*Hebrews*, 1:434].

28. Owen, *Works*, 18:445 [*Hebrews*, 1:445].

29. Giles Fletcher, *Israel Redux: or the Restauration of Israel* (London, 1677), title page, 119–22. For Lee, see T. G. Crippen, "Dr. Watts's Church Book," *Transactions of the Congregational Historical Society* 1 (1901–1904): 26–38; Peter Toon, *God's Statesman: The Life and Work of John Owen* (Exeter, UK: Paternoster, 1971), 152.

individuals associated with his congregation, including *The True Idea of Jansenisme* (1669), by Theophilus Gale, alongside whom Lee was preaching when *Israel Redux* was published. Owen would have repudiated Lee's interest in date setting but not his exuberant expectation of the dramatic changes that would accompany the coming of the kingdom. Owen's expectation of latter-day glory was global: although the Jews were "not called," "Antichrist not destroyed, the nations of the world generally wrapped up in idolatry and false worship, little dreaming of their deliverance," Christ would not "leave the world in this state, and set up his kingdom here on a molehill."[30] Owen was certain of the inexorable but gracious growth of Christ's "peaceable kingdom."[31]

It was hard to trace the growth of that "peaceable kingdom" in the horrific circumstances of the 1660s. As the new regime took control, supporters of the old republic were hunted down, arrested, and occasionally subjected to public and brutal displays of state power. Several of Owen's close associates were among those hung, drawn, and quartered in 1660–1661. The heads and limbs of those killed in these spectacles of sanctioned violence were displayed around London for the next several decades, and government spies discovered Owen consorting with other deprived ministers "in ye Fields on ye left hand neer Moregate where ye Quarters hang."[32] In 1662, the Act of Uniformity drove more than two thousand nonconforming ministers from the established church, creating the new community of dissent. It was easy for those feeling the full force of state opposition to interpret the Fire of London

---

30. Owen, *Works*, 8:376.
31. Owen, *Works*, 8:260.
32. Quoted in Crawford Gribben, *John Owen and English Puritanism: Experiences of Defeat*, Oxford Studies in Historical Theology (Oxford: Oxford University Press, 2016), 225.

and the devastation of plague as evidences of God's judgment against the nation.

In this tense and difficult period, Owen's eschatology also seems to have radicalized. Since Augustine, with hardly any exceptions, the Western church had understood the one-thousand-year binding of Satan described in Revelation 20 as a description either of the first millennium of Christian history or as a metaphor for the entire history of the church. This was the catholic consensus that had shaped Owen's earlier lack of interest in millennial theory. But in *A Brief Declaration and Vindication of the Doctrine of the Trinity* (1669), Owen changed position, arguing that Satan's binding—and therefore the millennium through which he would be bound—was to be expected in the future. Looking around him, at the horrific persecution of dissenters and at God's judgments of fire and plague, Owen regarded Satan as being "unweary and restless," as "neither conqueror nor conquered," adding, "nor will [he] be so, until he is bound and cast into the lake that burneth with fire."[33] Owen understood that the evils of Restoration England were proof positive that Satan was alive and well—and therefore that the millennium had yet to begin.

Through it all, Owen retained his expectation that Protestant Christianity would expand globally, even when he could see little evidence of that growth. If anything, he grew more pessimistic about the times in which he was living. He was discouraged by the state of the dissenting churches, too many of which seemed to be sitting lightly on the theological claims that he and others had hammered out in complex scholarship and exact confessions of faith. The churches were failing. Dissenters appeared to have "grown altogether indifferent as to the doctrine of God's eternal election, the sovereign efficacy of grace in

---

33. Owen, *Works*, 2:371.

the conversion of sinners, justification by the imputation of the righteousness of Christ," and they were even uncertain about the "interest of works in justification."[34] It was as if his long career of writing, preaching, and suffering had accomplished nothing of enduring value.

Owen's concerns were exacerbated by his inability to "know the times." His providential interpretation of history had enabled his sometimes quite radical take on the English Civil Wars: he had felt confident about tracing God's hand in human affairs while his own side was winning, in the 1640s and early to mid-1650s. But as he surveyed the troubled and sometimes dangerous days of the 1660s and 1670s, he worried that his interpretive method might be wrong. He knew that God had a controversy against the dissenters, but he could not explain why: "I do not know . . . a greater rebuke, in the whole course of my ministry, than that I have been labouring in the fire to discover the causes of God's withdrawing from us without any success."[35]

Owen was losing more than just his confidence. By the early 1680s, he had buried each of his ten children and his first wife. Despite Owen's eight million words and eighty published works, the theological culture of dissent was beginning to collapse. It was becoming increasingly apparent that Charles II would be replaced by his brother, the openly Catholic Duke of York, whose interest in religious freedom was widely understood as a bid to ensure liberty of worship for his co-religionists and whose ambition in statecraft was to emulate the absolutism of his cousin, Louis XIV of France. In December 1681, Owen was recognizing his weakness: "No man, I think, hath less of faith than I,— no man doth more despond."[36] By September 1682, it was clear

34. Owen, *Works*, 9:327, 459.
35. Owen, *Works*, 16:492.
36. Owen, *Works*, 9:6, 13, 15.

to Owen that England had abandoned the gains of the revolution, and the achievements of the Reformation seemed more than ever to be at risk. He admitted that he would never experience the latter-day glory he had long predicted: "I have wished sometimes I could live to see it," he considered, "but I do not think I shall."[37] With the nation in crisis and the churches in ruin, Owen turned his attention to spiritual life in another world.

Death

Owen was no stranger to death. He buried his first three children in the 1640s and three more in the following decade. As an adult, he had never been robustly healthy, and in March 1656, reports circulated that he was "neare death."[38] In the early 1660s, he must have been horrified by the spectacles of death and dismemberment as the Restoration government pursued and punished those it deemed particularly responsible for the trial and execution of Charles I. Even if Owen's handwriting remained fairly steady across the second half of his life, the contrast between the portrait created when Owen was vice-chancellor of the University of Oxford, sometime in the 1650s, and that created by Robert Walker in 1668 offers some evidence of his shrinking and much-diminished appearance. In the sermons that his listeners recorded in the 1660s and 1670s, his preaching was urgent, because he believed that life was short: "I speak to dying men, that know not how soon they may die. God advise my own heart of this thing, that I should labour and watch, that death might not find me out of the view of spiritual things."[39]

---

37. Owen, *Works*, 9:453.
38. *The Diary of Ralph Josselin*, ed. Alan Macfarlane, Records of Social and Economic History, n.s., 3 (Oxford: British Academy by the Oxford University Press, 1976), 363; *Report on the Manuscripts of the Earl of Egmont*, vol. 1, pt. 2, Historical Manuscripts Commission 2570 (London: Mackie for His Majesty's Stationery Office, 1905), 576.
39. Owen, *Works*, 9:352.

Owen understood death as an experience that often clarified the existence and achievements of spiritual life. He recognized that the evidences of spiritual life were often ambiguous and that "there are no professors but in distresses & on their death beds will applie to themselves . . . the promises of ye consoler of the spirit," even though these promises belong only to true believers.[40] Death often brought to light reality. When individuals were thrown onto their last resources, they showed where their true hopes lay. Owen remembered encouraging accounts of "young people who at their death have made a worke apparent in them from their infancy which was not before observed."[41] But the most encouraging accounts of death were those that held absolutely no ambiguity about the individual's experience of grace. No sight compared with that of a "poore dying [saint's] triumph over sinne & hell," Owen suggested; it was a "spectacle" that all believers would "desire above all but to see."[42] After all, for the Christian, with weak faith or strong, death was a "blessed thing," the "entrance into perfect joy."[43]

Owen's experience of joy seemed to be deferred. Around 1670, in addition to his political and pastoral concerns, he was beginning to feel old. He reported "daily warnings from my age, being now about fifty four[,] and many infirmities to be preparing for my dissolution."[44] In 1674, drawing on his experience of the deaths of nearly all his children, Owen counseled a grieving mother and a member of his congregation, Lady Elizabeth Hartopp, "Your dear infante is in the eternal enjoyment of the fruits of all our prayers; for the covenant of God is ordered

---

40. Notebook of Lucy Hutchinson, DD/HU3, 214–13 [reverse pagination on ms], Inspire Nottinghamshire Archives.
41. Notebook of Lucy Hutchinson, DD/HU3, 226, Inspire Nottinghamshire Archives.
42. Notebook of Lucy Hutchinson, DD/HU3, 202, Inspire Nottinghamshire Archives.
43. Notebook of Lucy Hutchinson, DD/HU3, 204, 205, Inspire Nottinghamshire Archives.
44. Owen to [Charles?] Nichols, in *The Correspondence of John Owen*, ed. Peter Toon (Cambridge: James Clarke, 1970), 148.

in all things and sure." Reflecting on his own experience, perhaps, or thinking of Elkanah's advice to Hannah (1 Sam. 1:8), he insisted that "God in Christ will be better to you than ten children."[45] In another undated letter, he wrote to the wife of Edward Polhill, for whose book *The Divine Will Considered in Its Eternal Decrees* (1673) Owen had contributed a preface. His counsel to Mrs. Polhill made no reference to the stern predestinarian theology of her husband's writing, nor to his qualified recommendation of her husband's views of the extent and intent of the atonement.[46] "Christ is your Pilott," he argued, returning to the nautical imagery that appears so frequently in his publications. "Sorrow not too much for the dead," he advised. The departed child had "entered into rest, and is taken away from the evill to come. Take heed lest, by too much griefe, you too much grieve the Holy Spirit, who is infinitely more to us than all natural relations." Owen was at his warmest when writing to grieving mothers. He assured Mrs. Polhill that "you are in my heart continually, which is nothing; but it helps to persuade me that you are in the heart of Christ, which is all."[47]

Owen's own griefs continued. He buried his wife, Mary, in 1677 and his last surviving daughter in 1682. Deaths continued within the membership of his increasingly elderly congregation. He was distressed by the deaths of prominent leaders among the Congregational churches. "Good ministers" were dying "almost every day," he lamented, and it was necessary that those who had benefited from their preaching should be prepared for the same fate. And so, as he entered what he

45. Owen to Lady Elizabeth Hartopp, in *Correspondence of John Owen*, 157–58; Crippen, "Dr. Watts's Church Book," 27.

46. John Owen, "The Preface to the Reader," in Edward Polhill, *The Divine Will Considered in Its Eternal Decrees* (London, 1673), n.p. This Mrs. Polhill does not appear to be the individual of the same name mentioned in Crippen, "Dr. Watts's Church Book," 27; J. William Black, "Edward Polhill," in *Oxford Dictionary of National Biography* (Oxford: Oxford University Press, 2004), s.v.

47. Owen to Mrs. Polhill, in *Correspondence of John Owen*, 168–69.

described as his "dying time," he began to prepare his congregation for their own deaths in a short sermon series on "dying daily" (1 Cor. 15:31).[48]

Owen's decision to preach this series of topical sermons was significant in terms of his changing homiletical practice. By 1680, he had largely abandoned the habit of preaching on a single passage or subject over multiple weeks, and this greater flexibility allowed him to narrow down more immediately on pressing needs among the Congregational churches. "It is the duty of all believers to be preparing themselves every day to die cheerfully, comfortably, and, if it may be, triumphing in the Lord," he insisted.[49] But every Christian could die with safety, even if every Christian did not have sufficient faith to die in peace.

Owen recognized the fears that death could bring. In his first sermon, he described death as the "entering into an invisible world," of which world the soul in this life could know nothing "but what it hath by faith."[50] The problem was, of course, that the Scriptures were curiously silent about the "invisible world." Owen, who had elsewhere debunked accounts of vampires and werewolves, took the occasion to explain to his congregation the origins of the ghost stories that were as popular in the late seventeenth century as they have been in any other period.[51] He wanted his listeners to focus on Scripture rather than superstition. And so, drawing on the exegetical work that he was continuing throughout this period, Owen considered what it meant to "die in faith" (Heb. 11:13). Turning on its head Paul's statement about faith, hope, and the en-

---

48. Owen, *Works*, 9:336.
49. Owen, *Works*, 9:336.
50. Owen, *Works*, 9:337.
51. Owen, *Works*, 9:338. Owen discusses vampires in *Theologoumena Pantodapa* (1661); see Owen, *Biblical Theology: The History of Theology from Adam to Christ*, trans. Stephen P. Westcott (Morgan, PA: Soli Deo Gloria, 1994), 133.

during power of love (1 Cor. 13:13), Owen argued that "love works, and hope works, and all other graces . . . work and help faith. But when we come to die, faith is left alone."[52]

These arguments were reinforced in the following week in the death of William Steele, a "great and eminent servant" of Christ whom Owen had known for thirty years and with whom he had been in church fellowship for fifteen years.[53] Owen felt the loss keenly. "The seat before my eyes is very much changed in a short time," he lamented.[54] And he wanted to persuade the rest of the congregation to be ready to follow him. While their minds were preoccupied by this bereavement, Owen directed his congregants to the daily practice of approaching God "as if you were immediately going into his presence, and into his hands," preparing to meet the angels who "carry the souls departed into Abraham's bosom."[55]

Owen completed his series on preparing for death with theological reflection. He recognized that "ever since it had a being," the soul had never had to experience life without the body to which it was attached.[56] He understood that an injury to the body, and especially serious and disabling head injuries, could have consequences for the "powers and faculties" of the soul.[57] He also understood how unique was the human apprehension about death. No other created being had two parts to its nature and had to face the prospect of their separation. Of all creation, only the making of humans involved the dust of the earth and the divine breath.[58] Angels were created as "pure, immaterial spirits" that "cannot die, from the principles

---

52. Owen, *Works*, 9:340.
53. Owen, *Works*, 9:341; Gribben, *John Owen and English Puritanism*, 258.
54. Owen, *Works*, 9:342.
55. Owen, *Works*, 20:253 [*Hebrews*, 3:253]; Owen, *Works*, 9:343–44.
56. Owen, *Works*, 9:346.
57. Owen, *Works*, 9:347.
58. Owen, *Works*, 9:348.

of [their] own constitution," while a "brute creature hath nothing in it that can live when death comes." But humans have
an "angelical nature from above that cannot die, and a nature
from beneath that cannot always live, since the entrance of sin,
though it might have done so before."[59] So when an individual
dies, Owen explained, "only one part of this nature continues
to act itself, according to its own powers."[60] The exercise of
preparing for death involved being ready to live without the
body, at least until the resurrection.

Preparing for death also involved being ready to live without
sin. Death was the final stage of the Christian's lifelong practice
of mortification. "Sin hath taken such a close, inseparable habitation in the body, that nothing but the death of the body can
make separation" from it, Owen explained. "There is no other
way to make an eternal separation between sin and the body
but by [the] consuming of it in the grave."[61] And when "all
other attempts to eradicate sin have failed," the faithful Christian would be "willing to part with [the] body" to be finally rid
of sin, so all-consuming was the desire for the full realization of
spiritual life.[62] For preparing for death also involved preparing
to be with Christ. "I have no inclination to be dissolved at the
end," Owen admitted, "but only as the means for another end,
that without it I cannot be with Christ."[63]

Resurrection and the Beatific Vision

It was the hope of being "with Christ" that sustained Owen
as national politics grew more threatening and as the condition of the dissenting churches continued to decline. As his

59. Owen, *Works*, 9:347.
60. Owen, *Works*, 9:348.
61. Owen, *Works*, 9:349.
62. Owen, *Works*, 9:350.
63. Owen, *Works*, 9:349.

health failed, he prepared for publication one of the last series of sermons that he preached to his congregation. The resulting book, *Meditations and Discourses on the Glory of Christ* (1684), offered an exposition of John 17:24. In his last months, and facing arrest on suspicion of his participation in seditious conspiracy, Owen recognized that dissenters found themselves in a "calamitous" situation:

> All things almost in all nations are filled with confusions, disorders, dangers, distresses, and troubles; wars and rumours of wars do abound, with tokens of farther approaching judgements; distress of nations, with perplexity, men's hearts failing them for fear, and looking after those things which are coming on the earth.

Many Christians were vexed with the "ungodly deeds of wicked men," which "doth greatly further the troubles of life," while others endured "deplorable" sufferings "for the testimony of their consciences," even as "divisions and animosities . . . abound amongst all sorts of Christians."[64] Worst of all, he feared, "never was there an age since the name of Christians was known upon the earth, wherein there was such a direct opposition made unto the Person and glory of Christ, as there is in that wherein we live."[65]

Meditations and Discourses on the Glory of Christ set out to defend the honor of its subject. It reconstructed the progress of grace in the Christian life around increasing views of the supremacy of Christ. "It is in Christ alone that we may have a clear, distinct view of the glory of God and his excellencies," Owen suggested, encouraging Christians to behold Christ by faith in order that they may one day do so by sight.[66]

---

64. Owen, *Works*, 1:278.
65. Owen, *Works*, 1:287.
66. Owen, *Works*, 1:299.

All Christians should understand the all-consuming pleasure of knowing the Lord Jesus, Owen insisted, because those who find in Christ "the life of present grace" will be those "unto whom he is the hope of future glory," in the culmination of spiritual life.[67]

This new emphasis on the glory of Christ caused Owen to reconsider his earlier views of the prophetic significance of the English Revolution. Forty years after the event, he could no longer attach prophetic significance to the revolution in which he had participated. In fact, he was no longer clear that Christians could properly exercise political power in the present age: "Some would reign here in this world; and we may say, with the apostles, 'Would you did reign, that we might reign with you.' But the members of the mystical body must be conformed unto the Head. In him sufferings went before glory; and so they must in them."[68] This was what explained the situation of dissenters in the 1670s and early 1680s, Owen argued. This was a suffering time—not a time for glory or for conquest but a time for bearing the cross.

Glory would come at the resurrection, when believers, simultaneously, would see Jesus "face to face," in renewed bodies.[69] With perfected, untiring bodies, and with minds and affections more capacious than ever before, "there will then be no satiety, no weariness, no indispositions; but the mind, being made perfect in all its faculties, powers, and operations, with respect unto its utmost end, which is the enjoyment of God, is satisfied in the beholding of him for evermore."[70] The beatific vision would be a vision of the humanity of Christ, Owen believed, in a sharp move away from the Thomistic tradition, which held

67. Owen, *Works*, 1:318.
68. Owen, *Works*, 1:343.
69. Owen, *Works*, 1:378.
70. Owen, *Works*, 1:406.

that believers would adore, in some abstract way, the divine essence. Believers were waiting for Jesus, Owen contended, and it was the incarnate and glorified Son who would forever be "admired in all them that believe" (2 Thess. 1:10). Christ "is, and shall be to eternity, the only means of communication between God and the church," for the "sight of God in Christ, which is intellectual, not corporeal; finite, not absolutely comprehensive of the divine essence; is the sum of our future blessedness."[71] Even in the eternal state, the divine essence will continue to be invisible to our glorified eyes and "uncomprehensible unto our minds." The "blessed and blessing sight which we shall have of God" will be always "in the face of Jesus Christ."[72] The final revelation, therefore, would be not the unveiling of politics, current affairs, or future scenarios of disaster or of earthly blessing but the unveiling of Jesus Christ. After a lifetime of work that most would have deemed a failure, and after failed eschatological hopes, Owen was waiting for Jesus.

Conclusion

"We know not how soon we may be called upon by death," Owen reflected in 1673, thinking about the "threescore years and ten" described in Psalm 90:10.[73] In the event, he did not reach that age. Ten years later, in late August 1683, at the age of sixty-eight, Owen was experiencing death for himself. He was more aware than he had been of its physical effects. He was in extreme discomfort. As he grew weaker, he wrote a letter by the hand of his wife to his old friend Charles Fleetwood, an army officer in the 1650s who had hosted the church in Stoke Newington in the decades thereafter. "I am very desirous to speak one word to you more in this world," Owen began. He

---

71. Owen, *Works*, 1:386; 24:287.
72. Owen, *Works*, 1:292.
73. Owen, *Works*, 9:351.

was finding his "dying hour" to be "irksome and wearisome through strong pains of various sorts which are all issued in an intermitting fever." His physical pain was exacerbated by the precarious situation of the dissenting churches. "I am leaving the ship of the church in a storm," he feared, with real concern about how well the community of dissenters would weather the changing political winds.[74] The achievements for which they had worked during the decade of revolution were no more than faded memories. One-quarter of a century after the death of Oliver Cromwell, Charles II was about to be succeeded by his brother James, the Duke of York, an outspoken Catholic who might bring, Owen and his peers feared, the final reversal of the English Reformation. English Protestantism might have no more enduring legacy than had the English Republic.

The situation was grave, but Owen was writing to encourage Fleetwood, despite their shared anxiety about the future. After all, he reflected, "whilst the great Pilot is in [the ship of the church] the loss of a poor under-rower will be inconsiderable. Live and pray and hope and waite patiently and doe not despair." Owen encouraged his old friend to remember that the "promise stands invincible that he will never leave thee nor forsake thee." Fleetwood could be sure that Owen was "going to him whom my soul hath loved, or rather who hath loved me with an everlasting love."[75] Owen was disappointed with the state of the dissenting churches and worried about the political direction of the country, but, understanding that "the world is a universal stranger unto the frame of children in their Father's house," Owen retained the happy expectation of heaven.[76] For the spiritual life that began in childhood would enter a significant new stage at death: "God hath a house and family for his

---

74. Owen to Charles Fleetwood, August 1683, in *Correspondence of John Owen*, 174.
75. Owen to Charles Fleetwood, August 1683, in *Correspondence of John Owen*, 174.
76. Owen, *Works*, 2:215.

children; of whom some he maintains on the riches of his grace, and some he entertains with the fulness of his glory" in the presence of Jesus Christ.[77] Owen was dying as a happy man. His attention was fixed on his glorified Savior, as an angel arrived to carry him to Abraham's bosom and God kissed out his soul.

---

77. Owen, *Works*, 2:208.

Conclusion

John Owen is widely recognized as the most important English Puritan writer—and perhaps the most important English theologian. His eight million words, published in eighty titles and across genres as distinctive as neo-Latin poetry, political commentary, New Testament exegesis, and scholastic theology, reflect the extraordinary achievements of his critical and creative mind. Owen's ideas were presented in books and pamphlets that were published over forty years, during a civil war, a revolutionary republic, and a return to monarchy that was catastrophic for Protestant dissenters. In these theological publications, he made a number of reversals that he did his best to conceal and, when necessary, defend. His bibliography also included some enduring spiritual classics, such as *Of Communion with God* (1657). But these theological publications do not represent the totality of his achievements, for Owen wrote other kinds of material as well. Taken as a whole, and read in biographical context, his published work seems diverse and cannot be adequately interpreted in the historical-theological approach that dominates Owen scholarship.

Owen's interests, which are suggested by the contents of his library, ranged far beyond theological ideas, and his publications went beyond the boundaries of the Western catholic tradition to reflect his concern about issues ranging from the proper nurture and education of children to the economic challenges faced by dissenters after the Restoration.[1] These were not, strictly speaking, theological issues, and so they have been largely sidelined in the voluminous bibliography of secondary sources that reconstruct and analyze his doctrinal arguments. But these issues were not somehow extraneous to Owen's main purpose. For all the work done by historical theologians, which has illuminated elements of Owen's thinking, some of it has in important ways underplayed his broader significance. Owen was interested in much more than theology—and these non-theological interests were often integral to his consideration of spiritual life.

Some readers may find this conclusion paradoxical—just as other readers may find paradoxical this book's rather positive focus on Owen's conception of spiritual life. The focus on Owen's theology was established during the recovery of interest in Puritan writing, which began in literature departments in American universities in the 1930s and picked up speed among popular reading audiences with the first publications of the Banner of Truth in the late 1950s. But while historical theologians have found this focus to be invigorating, scholars in other disciplines have found it to be oppressive and have on occasion traced that sense of oppression back into the primary sources.

So, for example, John Stachniewski's *The Persecutory Imagination: English Puritanism and the Literature of Religious Despair* (1991) argues that English Puritans combined Calvinist theology with a distinctive emphasis on conversion, much to

---

1. The catalog that was prepared for the posthumous auction of the contents of Owen's library must, however, be used with caution; see Crawford Gribben, "John Owen, Renaissance Man? The Evidence of Edward Millington's *Bibliotheca Oweniana* (1684)," *Westminster Theological Journal* 72, no. 2 (2010): 321–32, reprinted in *The Ashgate Research Companion to John Owen's Theology*, ed. Kelly M. Kapic and Mark Jones (Aldershot, UK: Ashgate, 2012), 97–109.

the danger of their impressionable readers and listeners.[2] Stachniewski observes, quite properly, that in Puritan salvific theory an individual's experience of conversion could be true or false and that the preachers and theologians who developed that theory exhorted their audiences to scrutinize themselves for evidences of eternal life. The result, he argues, was the production of a literature of despair, in which assurance of salvation was constantly undermined, leading in turn to a marked increase in religious despair and instances of suicide. In emphasizing these disastrous psychological consequences, instances of which are occasionally reported in Puritan writing, *The Persecutory Imagination* illustrates what may happen when scholars write about theology in the abstract and outside the lived experiences in which it is produced. Ironically, Stachniewski's foundational assumption, that Puritanism can be reduced to theological ideas, is reinforced in much of the historical-theological scholarship that interprets Owen's work.

More recently, scholars have opened up other aspects of the emotional life of English Puritans and have pushed beyond the gloomy stereotyping that once dominated the field. *Puritanism and Emotion in the Early Modern World* (2016), a volume edited by Alec Ryrie and Tom Schwanda, includes three chapters on happiness, while Tim Cooper's recent work on Richard Baxter has considered his contribution to discussions of human flourishing.[3] This approach needs to be developed within Owen scholarship. As unexpected as it may be, given his quite extraordinary experience of family bereavement, political defeat, and

---

2. John Stachniewski, *The Persecutory Imagination: English Puritanism and the Literature of Religious Despair* (Oxford: Clarendon, 1991).

3. Alec Ryrie and Tom Schwanda, eds., *Puritanism and Emotion in the Early Modern World*, Christianities in the Trans-Atlantic World, 1500–1800 (Basingstoke, UK; Palgrave Macmillan, 2016); Tim Cooper, "Richard Baxter and Human Flourishing: Future Rest Assured," The Commonweal Project, April 29, 2017, https://thecommonweal project.org/2017/04/29/richard-baxter-and-human-flourishing-future-rest-assured/.

ecclesiastical disappointment, and his own encounter with depression, Owen's emphasis was on the joyful possibilities held out by spiritual life. "You know how unwilling we are to part with anything we have labored and beaten our heads about?" he asked of his readers. He continued,

> When once Christ appears to the soul, when he is known in his excellency, all these things . . . have their paint washed off, their beauty fades, their desirableness vanisheth, and the soul is not only contented to part with them all, but puts them away as a defiled thing, and cries, "In the Lord Jesus only is my righteousness and glory."[4]

As this emotional response suggests, Owen was much more than a theological clinician, and future work on his depiction of spiritual life will need to be more holistic in scope.

Owen's interest in spiritual life went far beyond the articulation of theological ideas. His conception of spiritual life began in childhood, continued though youth, maturity, and death, and was consummated in the beatific vision of the glory of God displayed in Jesus Christ. It united into a single narrative his arguments about God as Trinity, the accomplishment and application of redemption, the fellowship of believers in the church, and the Christian's expectation of future glory. And it fully engaged with the social, cultural, and political contexts of its production. Owen considered what Christian responsibility might look like in the home, in the church, and in an often hostile world. And, as this book argues, Owen's discussion of spiritual life has contributed, and perhaps even shaped, some of the most important religious communities and political philosophies of the last several centuries of civilization in the West. Owen was so much more than merely the most important English theologian.

---

4. Owen, *Works*, 2:138.

The Formation of Classical Liberalism

One unintended consequence of Owen's discussion of spiritual life was the formation of classical liberalism—an ideology that since the later seventeenth century has emphasized the rights and responsibilities of citizens and governments, upholding private property under the rule of law, thus to dominate the political culture of the English-speaking world. In the decades that followed his death in 1683, Owen's legacy was more obvious in political than in theological contexts. While he died lamenting the erosion of orthodoxy among Protestant dissenters, which his doctrinal treatises could not stem, his work to promote the toleration of Protestant dissenters was ultimately successful. His best arguments were taken up in the debate in and after the later 1680s, around the time of the Glorious Revolution, in which Locke's *Two Treatises of Government* (1689) became the best-known interventions. Owen's thinking about Christian living had developed to address some important shortcomings in the Reformed tradition—and the fact that this claim sounds so peculiar is evidence of how successful his rewriting of the Reformed tradition has been.

Owen was no mere ventriloquist of the Calvinist Reformation. The theological tradition that he inherited had fashioned a more or less common confession, which appeared with some important variety of emphasis and sometimes with some surprising inclusions and omissions, across scores of statements of faith.[5] But this was not the confession that he passed on. While he offered minor adjustments to some doctrines, as in his emphasis on double imputation in justification, and added

---

5. Chris Caughey and Crawford Gribben, "History, Identity Politics, and the 'Recovery of the Reformed Confession,'" in Matthew C. Bingham, Chris Caughey, R. Scott Clark, Crawford Gribben, and D. G. Hart, *On Being Reformed: Debates over a Theological Identity*, Christianities in the Trans-Atlantic World (Basingstoke, UK: Palgrave, 2018), 1–26.

significant detail to others, as in his extended discussion of the person and work of the Holy Spirit, Owen entirely abandoned the assumption common to earlier Reformed confessions that the state should serve the purposes of the church and be governed by divine law.

Instead, Owen argued that the state should tolerate a broad range of religious opinions—though never all religious opinions. He advanced this argument in publications from the later 1640s until the end of his life. But he articulated this argument in ways that reflected his changing situation. His earlier assertions of this argument were made mostly while he was in a position of influence, in which he was prepared to graciously tolerate others who enjoyed less official favor than himself. His later assertions of this argument were made mostly while he faced legal jeopardy and depended on others to tolerate him.

After the Restoration, Owen was compelled to think carefully about the nature of Christian pilgrimage during the "time of [our] sojourning" (1 Pet. 1:17). In political terms, he moved away from the Constantinian politics of the Reformed confessions of faith to adopt instead a post-Constantinian politics. He no longer assumed that believers could advance God's purposes by means of political power. He no longer faced the temptation to "immanentize the eschaton" but began to recognize his duty to "look," or wait, for Jesus (Phil. 3:20). His agenda was no longer to control the state but to find a political philosophy that could ensure his being tolerated by the state. And so, he came to realize, the spiritual life that he idealized required the toleration of others whose religious opinions differed from his. Many of Owen's most significant contemporaries shared these assumptions and, like Locke, gradually worked their way toward his conclusions.

The result of this protracted debate was that the religious settlement of the Glorious Revolution was essentially the settlement for which Owen had been arguing for the previous forty years—and more emphatically than ever in the aftermath of the Restoration. Owen's consideration of how Christians should contribute to their society threw up the question of reciprocal rights and generated a compelling and persuasive account of religious toleration, which by means of its interpretation by Locke and its widespread dissemination during the American Revolution has come to dominate Western ideas about liberty. The first of the unintended consequences of Owen's thinking about spiritual life may be found in the politics of classical liberalism.

The Formation of Evangelicalism

A second unintended consequence of Owen's discussion of spiritual life was the formation of the approach to religion that in the early twenty-first century has come to dominate global Protestantism. It is true that Owen's own congregation came to tolerate the Trinitarian experimentation of theologians like Isaac Watts, whom some London Unitarians believed should be counted among their number, and it is also true that the communities within English dissent that most valued his contribution came to so emphasize the divine decrees that they disengaged from the world and entered a long period of myopic introversion. Yet Owen's ideas of spiritual life were not forgotten. Owen's new readers appeared in unexpected contexts in the movement that evolved out of English Puritanism and that came to public attention on both sides of the Atlantic in the religious revivals of the 1730s and 1740s. The leaders of evangelicalism, as this new religious movement was known, eagerly appropriated Owen's emphasis on individual spiritual experience, which they promoted often without proper consideration of his sometimes rather weak emphasis on the importance of the church.

The new evangelical movement proposed an account of popular Protestantism that grew on both sides of the Atlantic through the eighteenth and nineteenth centuries. In England and in America, the leaders of evangelicalism moved increasingly away from the norms of the Reformed tradition, even as they maintained the emphasis on individual piety that they found in Owen's work. In the eighteenth century, Owen was republished by John Wesley but less often by Wesley's followers. In the nineteenth century, Owen's ecclesiological works and his massive and extraordinarily learned commentary on Hebrews were republished in Scotland, while publishers in England and America preferred to sell his less technical and more devotional contributions. Over one century after his death, Owen's fate, it appeared, was to be used to validate the special interests of his readers.

By the mid-nineteenth century, however, Owen was being identified as the Puritan writer whose work defined evangelicalism. In 1844, the well-known artist John Rogers Herbert completed the best-known visualization of the work of the most important ecclesiastical body in seventeenth-century Protestantism. Herbert was a convert to Catholicism, but his representation of the Westminster Assembly sought to turn the body into a talisman of early Victorian ideals of liberty. He added to the members of the assembly three individuals who never attended its meetings—John Milton, Oliver Cromwell, and John Owen. Their addition was not merely anachronistic. Herbert was making a point—for Owen, at least in popular imagination, was now central to "the assertion of liberty of conscience by the Independents at the Westminster Assembly of Divines" and to the validation of evangelical religion in general.

Owen was a crucial interlocutor for evangelicals in the later nineteenth century as they continued to move away from the conventions of the Reformed tradition. Though he received less attention in the early twentieth century, he was never entirely forgotten. In the mid-twentieth century, when he was rediscovered by men who would be central to the modern recovery of Reformed theology, including D. Martyn Lloyd-Jones, and republished by the organizations that would do the most to promote that recovery, including Banner of Truth, Owen began to attract a much larger popular readership than ever before. Across denominations and on both sides of the Atlantic, Owen's readership grew as publishers reprinted ever-increasing numbers of his books, sometimes in modernized English, thus consolidating and expanding his readership among the "young, restless, and Reformed."[6] Owen was back in fashion, and his ideas mattered more than ever before. In 2009, *Time* magazine featured a cover story in which "the new Calvinism," which the republication of Owen had done so much to facilitate, was identified as one of ten ideas that were changing the world.[7] Owen had lived in the expectation that Reformed Protestantism would become globalized. Had he lived into the twenty-first century, he might have understood the extent of his contribution to it. His work now shapes the spiritual lives of millions of readers.

A Final Word

Owen was an appreciative legatee of the Western catholic tradition and the insights of the Reformation, which meant that his

---

6. Collin Hansen, *Young, Restless, Reformed: A Journalist's Journey with the New Calvinists* (Wheaton, IL: Crossway, 2008).

7. David Van Biema, "10 Ideas Changing the World Right Now: The New Calvinism," *Time*, March 12, 2009.

understanding of spiritual life was thoroughly theological; and he was a constant student of Scripture, which meant that his conclusions developed over time. In several respects, as we have seen, his discussion of spiritual life came to modify standard elements of early modern Reformed theology. In religious terms, his work in theology and church life and his increasing focus on individual spirituality moved some significant distance from the conclusions of his contemporaries, Presbyterian and Congregational alike, to provide a critical foundation for the approach to religion that is now promoted in global evangelicalism.

Owen's understanding of grace was perhaps clearest after his experience of defeat. After the Restoration, his political thinking took account of the transience of power, as it recognized the minority status of dissenters in a world in which they had few rights. After Owen was thrown back onto the mercy of the former victims of the Cromwellian regime, his work in politics backtracked from the uncritical celebration of the revolution to developing a view of church-state relations that was much more cautious in its expectations of civil government. This move facilitated the ideas about toleration that he formulated in the 1650s and restated with increasing conviction in the 1660s and that were slowly adopted by his most famous former student, John Locke, by means of whom they became foundational to classical liberalism and therefore to the formation of Western democracy.

Owen was, by any measure, an outstanding theologian—though he was more than that. Following the conventions of the Reformed theological tradition with which he identified, and drawing on a literature that included Thomas Aquinas and Augustine as much as John Calvin and Paul, he understood that the Christian life progressed from grace to grace (John

1:16) and from grace to glory (Ps. 84:11).[8] His construction of the Christian life was grounded in his doctrine of progressive sanctification and his convictions about true believers' perseverance in the life of faith. But his contribution to the Calvinist Reformation, classical liberalism, and the emergence of evangelicalism represents only a part of his achievement. For his genius was to wrap up discussions of theological minutiae with questions of compelling and enduring political importance in one of the most wide-ranging discussions of grace, goodness, and spiritual life.

---

8. This point has been elucidated in Sinclair B. Ferguson, *John Owen on the Christian Life* (Edinburgh: Banner of Truth, 1987); Matthew Barrett and Michael A. G. Haykin, *Owen on the Christian Life: Living for the Glory of God in Christ*, Theologians on the Christian Life (Wheaton, IL: Crossway, 2015).

Appendix

Prayers for Children from John Owen, *The Primer* (1652)

The Desiring of a Blessing before Meat

Holy Father, thou taketh care of us, and provideth for us, and we live continually upon thy allowance, in our selves we have neither hope nor help: we pray thee give us to taste of thy love and kindesse in the creatures thou hast now prepared for us; command a blessing upon them, and let the blessing of thy free Grace be upon our hearts to prepare them for thy selfe, and thy service, through Jesus Christ our Lord.

A Thanksgiving after Meat

Thou reneweth thy mercies unto us, O Lord; because great is thy faithfulnesse: make our hearts, we pray thee, sensible of thy goodnesse and kindnesse towards us, and teach us in the injoyment of thy manifold mercies, to live unto thy praise, through Jesus Christ our Lord.

A Prayer for the Morning

Blessed Lord God, the God and Father of our Lord and Saviour Jesus Christ: and in him my God, and my Father, of whose patience and mercy it is that I am not consumed; I thy poor creature, and unworthy sinful servant, do beseech thee to lift up the light of thy countenance upon me, and to make me accepted in thy beloved Son: wash me in his blood from all my sins and defilements, and make him to be Righteousness unto me, who have none in myself: O Lord, I am weak, dark, and ignorant, give me to know thee, the onely true God, and whom thou hast sent, Jesus Christ: fill my heart with the feare of thy great Name, and help me to grow up, and to increase in grace, and in the knowledge of my Lord and Saviour: let me not be led aside into the snares of Satan, and paths of ungodlinesse, to be a griefe unto thy Spirit, or a provocation to the eye of thy glory: Be with me this day, whereunto in thy patience and forbearance thou hast brought me: keep me from sin and danger, help me to perform the duties thou requirest at my hands, and the things that I know not, do thou teach me. Bless all thine own people everywhere with an increase of Grace and Peace: establish the Common-Wealth of this nation in righteousness and quietnesse; let thy Gospel yet flourish amongst us; deal with my parents and friends, as thou usest to deal with them that fear thy Name, and be my God, and my guide all my days, through Jesus Christ my Lord.

A Prayer for the Evening

Most holy Lord God, and in Jesus Christ the Father of mercy, and the God of all consolation, thou hearest the desires of them who draw nigh to the throne of Grace, through the new and living way which thou hast appointed, to make their requests known unto thee with supplications: I thy poore sinful creature do beseech thee in Jesus Christ, to stretch out thy Fatherly armes unto my soule, to receive it with mercy into thy bosom-love. It is the riches of thy Grace alone that I desire to roll myself upon; for in myself I am sinful, defiled, unbelieving, so that thou mighteth justly cast me out of thy presence for evermore: but there is mercy and forgiveness with thee that thou mayest be feared: O let my soul have a share therein: thou hast been good unto me the day past, take me now this night into thy blessed care and protection, let me know thee more, and love thee more, and trust thee more by working of that love of thine, which thou showest in the mercies of the morning and evening, through that my Lord and Saviour. Amen.

Another Prayer

Blessed God, and my dear Father in Jesus Christ, I beseech thee to give me thy holy Spirit to dwell in me, and to bring my soul unto thee: let the Lord Jesus be my lot and portion, and my heart be filled with the feare of thy great Name: show me, O Lord, thy kindnesse, even in the things of this life, and let my poor soul be always precious in thy sight, through Christ our Lord.

Bibliography

This bibliography updates the bibliography included in Crawford Gribben, *John Owen and English Puritanism: Experiences of Defeat*, Oxford Studies in Historical Theology (Oxford: Oxford University Press, 2016), 352–85.

Manuscripts

British Library, London: BL Sloane 3680, Sermons by Dr. Owen, Mr. Perrott, and Others, 1672–1675.

Dr. Williams's Library, London: NCL/L6/2–4, Notebook of Sir John Hartopp.

Inspire Nottinghamshire Archives: DD/HU3, Notebook of Lucy Hutchinson.

Oxford, Bodleian Library: MS Don. f. 40, fols. 113–17, Notebook of Thomas Aldersey.

University of Edinburgh, New College: MS Comm. 1, Notebook of Smith Fleetwood.

Primary Sources

Asty, John. "Memoirs of the Life of John Owen, D.D." In *A Complete Collection of the Sermons of the Reverend and Learned John Owen, D.D.* London, 1721.

Baillie, Robert. *The Letters and Journals of Robert Baillie, 1637–1662.* Edited by David Laing. Edinburgh: Robert Ogle, 1841–1842.

Burgess, Cornelius. *Baptismall Regeneration of Elect Infants Professed by the Church of England, according to the Scriptures, the Primitive Church, the Present Reformed Churches, and Many Particular Divines Apart.* Oxford, 1629.

Calvin, John. *Institutes of the Christian Religion.* Edited by John T. McNeill. Translated by Ford Lewis Battles. Philadelphia, PA: Westminster Press, 1960.

Clarkson, David. "A Funeral Sermon of the Much Lamented Death of the Late Reverend and Learned Divine John Owen, D.D." In *Seventeen Sermons Preach'd by the Late Reverend and Learned John Owen, D.D.* 2 vols. London, 1720.

The Clergy of the Church of England Database. http://theclergy database.org.uk.

Crippen, T. G. "Dr. Watts's Church Book." *Transactions of the Congregational Historical Society* 1 (1901–1904): 26–38.

Cromwell, Henry. *The Correspondence of Henry Cromwell, 1655–1659.* Edited by Peter Gaunt. Camden Fifth Series 31. Cambridge: Cambridge University Press, 2007.

Cromwell, Oliver. *The Writings and Speeches of Oliver Cromwell.* Edited by W. C. Abbott. 4 vols. Cambridge, MA: Harvard University Press, 1947.

Crosfield, Thomas. *The Diary of Thomas Crosfield.* Edited by Frederick S. Boas. London: Oxford University Press, 1935.

An Elegy on the Death of That Learned, Pious, and Famous Divine, Doctor John Owen. London, 1683.

Firth, C. H., and R. S. Rait, eds. *Acts and Ordinances of the Interregnum, 1642–1660.* 3 vols. London: His Majesty's Stationery Office, 1911.

Fletcher, Giles. *Israel Redux: or the Restauration of Israel.* London, 1677.

Humble Proposals concerning the Printing of the Bible. London, 1650.

Hutchinson, Lucy. *Memoirs of the Life of Colonel Hutchinson, Governor of Nottingham*. Revised and edited by C. H. Firth. 2 vols. London: J. M. Dent, 1885, 1906.

———. *On the Principles of the Christian Religion, Addressed to Her Daughter; and On Theology*. London, 1817.

———. *Order and Disorder*. Edited by David Norbrook. Oxford: Blackwell, 2001.

———. *The Works of Lucy Hutchinson*. Vol. 2, *Theological Writings and Translations*, edited by Elizabeth Clarke, David Norbrook, and Jane Stevenson, with textual introductions by Jonathan Gibson and editorial assistance from Mark Burden and Alice Eardley. Oxford: Oxford University Press, 2018.

Johnston, Archibald. *The Diary of Sir Archibald Johnston of Wariston*. Edited by D. H. Fleming. 3 vols. Edinburgh: Scottish History Society, 1919–1940.

Josselin, Ralph. *The Diary of Ralph Josselin*. Edited by Alan Macfarlane. Records of Social and Economic History, n.s., 3. Oxford: British Academy by the Oxford University Press, 1976.

Locke, John. *The Correspondence of John Locke*, edited by E. S. de Beer. 8 vols. In *The Clarendon Edition of the Works of John Locke*, edited by M. A. Stewart, Peter Nidditch, and John Yolton. Oxford: Clarendon, 1976.

———. *An Essay concerning Toleration, and Other Writings on Law and Politics, 1667–1683*, edited by J. R. Milton and Philip Milton. In *The Clarendon Edition of the Works of John Locke*, edited by M. A. Stewart, Peter Nidditch, and John Yolton. Oxford: Clarendon, 2006.

———. *Political Writings*. Edited by David Wootton. London: Penguin, 1993.

Millington, Edward. *Bibliotheca Oweniana*. London, 1684.

Orme, William. *Memoirs of the Life, Writings, and Religious Connexions, of John Owen, D.D., Vice-Chancellor of Oxford and*

Dean of Christ Church, during the Commonwealth. London: T. Hamilton, 1820.

———. "Memoirs of the Life and Writings of Dr. John Owen." In vol. 1 of *The Works of John Owen*, edited by Thomas Russell, xix–cxxii. London: Paternoster, 1826.

Owen, John. *Biblical Theology: The History of Theology from Adam to Christ*. Translated by Stephen P. Westcott. Morgan, PA: Soli Deo Gloria, 1994.

———. *The Correspondence of John Owen*. Edited by Peter Toon. Cambridge: James Clarke, 1970.

———. "Dr. Owen to the Reader." In Henry Scudder, *The Christians Daily Walk*, n.p. London, 1674.

———. *The Oxford Orations of John Owen*. Edited by Peter Toon. Callington, Cornwall, UK: Gospel Communications, 1971.

———. *The Primer*. London, 1652.

———. *The Works of John Owen*. Edited by William H. Goold. 24 vols. Edinburgh: Johnstone and Hunter, 1850–1855.

Polhill, Edward. *The Divine Will Considered in Its Eternal Decrees*. London, 1673.

Report on the Manuscripts of the Earl of Egmont. Vol. 1, pt. 2. Historical Manuscripts Commission 2570. London: Mackie for His Majesty's Stationery Office, 1905.

Rush, Benjamin. "To Thomas Jefferson from Benjamin Rush, 6 October 1800." In *The Papers of Thomas Jefferson*. Vol. 32, *1 June 1800 to 16 February 1801*, edited by Barbara B. Oberg, 204–7. Princeton, NJ: Princeton University Press, 2005.

[The Savoy Declaration.] *A Declaration of the Faith and Order owned and practiced in the Congregational Churches in England; Agreed upon and consented unto by their elders and messengers in their meeting at the Savoy* (London, 1658).

Thorseby, Ralph. *The Diary of Ralph Thorseby, F.R.S.* Edited by Joseph Hunter. 2 vols. London, 1830.

A Vindication of the Late Reverend and Learned John Owen D.D. London, 1684.

[Westminster Assembly.] *A Directory for the Publique Worship of God throughout the Three Kingdomes of England, Scotland, and Ireland.* London, 1645.

Secondary Sources

Barraclough, Peter. *John Owen, 1616–1683.* London: Independent Press, 1961.

Barrett, Matthew, and Michael A. G. Haykin. *Owen on the Christian Life: Living for the Glory of God in Christ.* Theologians on the Christian Life. Wheaton, IL: Crossway, 2015.

Bennett, Martyn. *The Civil Wars in Britain and Ireland, 1638–1651.* Oxford: Blackwell, 1997.

Bill, E. G. W. *Education at Christ Church, Oxford, 1660–1800.* Oxford: Clarendon, 1988.

Bingham, Matthew C., Chris Caughey, R. Scott Clark, Crawford Gribben, and D. G. Hart. *On Being Reformed: Debates over a Theological Identity.* Christianities in the Trans-Atlantic World. Basingstoke, UK: Palgrave, 2018.

Boersma, Hans. *Seeing God: The Beatific Vision in Christian Tradition.* Grand Rapids, MI: Eerdmans, 2018.

———. "Thomas Aquinas on the Beatific Vision: A Christological Deficit." *TheoLogica: An International Journal for Philosophy of Religion and Philosophical Theology* 2, no. 2 (2018), accessed April 23, 2019, https://ojs.uclouvain.be/index.php/theologica/article/view/14733.

Cambers, Andrew. *Godly Reading: Print, Manuscript and Puritanism in England, 1580–1720.* Cambridge Studies in Early Modern British History. Cambridge: Cambridge University Press, 2011.

Caughey, Chris, and Crawford Gribben. "History, Identity Politics, and the 'Recovery of the Reformed Confession.'" In

Matthew C. Bingham, Chris Caughey, R. Scott Clark, Crawford Gribben, and D. G. Hart, *On Being Reformed: Debates over a Theological Identity*, 1–26. Christianities in the Trans-Atlantic World. Basingstoke, UK: Palgrave, 2018.

Caughey, Christopher Earl. "Puritan Responses to Antinomianism in the Context of Reformed Covenant Theology, 1630–1696." PhD diss., Trinity College Dublin, 2013.

Chapman, Alister, John Coffey, and Brad S. Gregory, eds. *Seeing Things Their Way: Intellectual History and the Return of Religion*. South Bend, IN: University of Notre Dame Press, 2009.

Clark, J. C. D. *English Society, 1688–1832: Ideology, Social Structure and Political Practice during the Ancien Regime*. Cambridge Studies in the History and Theory of Politics. Cambridge: Cambridge University Press, 1985.

Clarke, Elizabeth. *Politics, Religion and the Song of Songs in Seventeenth-Century England*. New York: Palgrave, 2011.

Cleveland, Christopher. *Thomism in John Owen*. Farnham, UK: Ashgate, 2013.

Coffey, John. *John Goodwin and the Puritan Revolution: Religion and Intellectual Change in Seventeenth-Century England*. Woodbridge, UK: Boydell, 2006.

———. "John Owen and the Puritan Toleration Controversy, 1646–59." In *The Ashgate Research Companion to John Owen's Theology*, edited by Kelly M. Kapic and Mark Jones, 227–48. Aldershot, UK: Ashgate, 2012.

———. "Lloyd-Jones and the Protestant Past." In *Engaging with Martyn Lloyd-Jones: The Life and Legacy of "the Doctor,"* edited by Andrew Atherstone and David Ceri Jones, 293–325. Nottingham, UK: Apollos, 2011.

———. *Politics, Religion and the British Revolutions: The Mind of Samuel Rutherford*. Cambridge Studies in Early Modern British History. Cambridge: Cambridge University Press, 1997.

———. "Puritan Legacies." In *The Cambridge Companion to Puritanism*, edited by John Coffey and Paul C.-H. Lim, 327–45. Cambridge: Cambridge University Press, 2008.

———. "Ticklish Business: Defining Heresy and Orthodoxy in the Puritan Revolution." In *Heresy, Literature and Politics in Early Modern English Culture*, edited by David Loewenstein and John Marshall, 108–36. Cambridge: Cambridge University Press, 2006.

———. "The Toleration Controversy during the English Revolution." In *Religion in Revolutionary England*, edited by Christopher Durston and Judith Maltby, 42–68. Manchester: Manchester University Press, 2006.

Cook, Sarah Gibbard. "A Political Biography of a Religious Independent: John Owen, 1616–1683." PhD diss., Harvard University, 1972.

Cooper, Tim. *Fear and Polemic in Seventeenth-Century England: Richard Baxter and Antinomianism*. Aldershot, UK: Ashgate, 2001.

———. *John Owen, Richard Baxter, and the Formation of Nonconformity*. Farnham, UK: Ashgate, 2011.

———. "Owen's Personality: The Man behind the Theology." In *The Ashgate Research Companion to John Owen's Theology*, edited by Kelly M. Kapic and Mark Jones, 215–26. Aldershot, UK: Ashgate, 2012.

———. "Richard Baxter and Human Flourishing: Future Rest Assured." The Commonweal Project, April 29, 2017. https://thecommonwealproject.org/2017/04/29/richard-baxter-and-human-flourishing-future-rest-assured/.

———. "State of the Field: 'John Owen Unleashed: Almost.'" *Conversations in Religion and Theology* 6, no. 2 (2008): 226–57.

———. "Why Did Richard Baxter and John Owen Diverge? The Impact of the First Civil War." *Journal of Ecclesiastical History* 61, no. 3 (2010): 496–516.

Cowan, Martyn C. *John Owen and the Civil War Apocalypse: Preaching, Prophecy and Politics*. New York: Routledge, 2018.

Dale, B. *The Annals of Coggeshall, Otherwise Sunnedon, in the County of Essex*. Coggeshall, 1863.

Daniels, Richard W. *The Christology of John Owen*. Grand Rapids, MI: Reformed Heritage Books, 2004.

Davis, J. C. "Cromwell's Religion." In *Oliver Cromwell and the English Revolution*, edited by John Morrill, 181–87. London: Longman, 1990.

de Vries, Peter. "The Significance of Union and Communion with Christ in the Theology of John Owen (1616–1683)." *Reformed Theological Journal* 17 (2001): 75–89.

———. "Union and Communion with Christ in the Theology of John Owen." *Reformed Theological Journal* 15 (1999): 77–96.

Dixon, Philip. *Nice and Hot Disputes: The Doctrine of the Trinity in the Seventeenth Century*. London: T&T Clark, 2003.

Durston, Christopher, and Judith Maltby, eds. *Religion in Revolutionary England*. Manchester: Manchester University Press, 2006.

Ferguson, Sinclair B. "John Owen and the Doctrine of the Holy Spirit." In *John Owen: The Man and His Theology*, edited by Robert W. Oliver, 101–30. Phillipsburg, NJ: P&R, 2002.

———. "John Owen and the Doctrine of the Person of Christ." In *John Owen: The Man and His Theology*, edited by Robert W. Oliver, 69–100. Phillipsburg, NJ: P&R, 2002.

———. *John Owen on the Christian Life*. Edinburgh: Banner of Truth, 1987.

———. *The Trinitarian Devotion of John Owen*. Sanford, FL: Reformation Trust, 2014.

Foord, Martin. "John Owen's Gospel Offer: Well-Meant or Not?" In *The Ashgate Research Companion to John Owen's Theology*, edited by Kelly M. Kapic and Mark Jones, 283–96. Aldershot, UK: Ashgate, 2012.

Ford, Alan. *James Ussher: Theology, History, and Politics in Early-Modern Ireland and England.* Oxford: Oxford University Press, 2007.

Gaine, Simon Francis. "Thomas Aquinas and John Owen on the Beatific Vision: A Reply to Suzanne McDonald." *New Blackfriars* 97, no. 1070 (2016): 432–46.

Gardiner, Samuel Rawson, ed. *The Constitution Documents of the Puritan Revolution, 1625–1660.* 3rd ed. Oxford: Clarendon, 1936.

———. *History of the Commonwealth and Protectorate, 1649–1656.* 4 vols. London: Longmans, Green, 1903.

Gatiss, Lee. "Adoring the Fullness of the Scriptures in John Owen's Commentary on Hebrews." PhD diss., University of Cambridge, 2014.

———. *From Life's First Cry: John Owen on Infant Baptism and Infant Salvation.* St. Antholin's Lectureship Charity Lecture 2008. London: Latimer Trust, 2008. Partially reprinted as "From Life's First Cry: John Owen on Infant Baptism and Infant Salvation." In *The Ashgate Research Companion to John Owen's Theology*, edited by Kelly M. Kapic and Mark Jones, 271–82. Aldershot, UK: Ashgate, 2012.

———. "Socinianism and John Owen." *Southern Baptist Journal of Theology* 20, no. 4 (2016): 43–62.

Gleason, Randall C. *John Calvin and John Owen on Mortification: A Comparative Study in Reformed Spirituality.* Studies in Church History 3. New York: Peter Lang, 1995.

Greaves, Richard. *John Bunyan and English Nonconformity.* London: Hambledon, 1992.

Greaves, Richard L., and Robert Zaller, eds. *Biographical Dictionary of British Radicals in the Seventeenth Century.* 3 vols. Brighton: Harvester, 1982–1984.

Gribben, Crawford. "Becoming John Owen: The Making of an Evangelical Reputation." *Westminster Theological Journal* 79, no. 2 (2017): 311–25.

———. "John Owen (1616–1683): Four Centuries of Influence." *Reformation Today* 273 (September–October 2016): 10–18.

———. "John Owen, Baptism, and the Baptists." In *By Common Confession: Essays in Honor of James M. Renihan*, edited by Ronald S. Baines, Richard C. Barcellos, and James P. Butler, 53–72. Palmdale, CA: Reformed Baptist Academic Press, 2015.

———. "John Owen, Renaissance Man? The Evidence of Edward Millington's *Bibliotheca Oweniana* (1684)." *Westminster Theological Journal* 72, no. 2 (2010): 321–32. Reprinted in *The Ashgate Research Companion to John Owen's Theology*, edited by Kelly M. Kapic and Mark Jones, 97–109. Aldershot, UK: Ashgate, 2012.

———. *John Owen and English Puritanism: Experiences of Defeat*. Oxford Studies in Historical Theology. Oxford: Oxford University Press, 2016.

———. "Poetry and Piety: John Owen, Faithful Teate and Communion with God." In *The Pure Flame of Devotion: The History of Christian Spirituality; Essays in Honour of Michael A. G. Haykin*, edited by G. Steven Weaver Jr. and Ian Hugh Clary, 197–215. Toronto, ON: Joshua Press, 2013.

———. "Polemic and Apocalyptic in the Cromwellian Invasion of Scotland." *Literature & History* 23, no. 1 (2014): 1–18.

———. *The Puritan Millennium: Literature and Theology, 1550–1682*. Dublin: Four Courts, 2000.

Griffiths, Steve. *Redeem the Time: Sin in the Writings of John Owen*. Fearn, Ross-shire, Scotland: Mentor, 2001.

Haigh, Christopher. "The Church of England, the Nonconformists and Reason: Another Restoration Controversy." *Journal of Ecclesiastical History* 69, no. 3 (2018): 531–56.

———. "'Theological Wars': 'Socinians' v. 'Antinomians' in Restoration England." *Journal of Ecclesiastical History* 67, no. 2 (2016): 325–50.

Halcomb, Joel. "A Social History of Congregational Religious Practice during the Puritan Revolution." PhD diss., University of Cambridge, 2010.

Hansen, Collin. *Young, Restless, Reformed: A Journalist's Journey with the New Calvinists*. Wheaton, IL: Crossway, 2008.

Haykin, Michael A. G. "The Calvin of England: Some Aspects of the Life of John Owen (1616–1683) and His Teaching on Biblical Piety." *Reformed Baptist Theological Review* 1, no. 2 (2004): 169–83.

———. "John Owen and the Challenge of the Quakers." In *John Owen: The Man and His Theology*, edited by Robert W. Oliver, 131–56. Phillipsburg, NJ: P&R, 2002.

Haykin, Michael A. G., and Mark Jones, eds. *Drawn into Controversie: Reformed Theological Diversity and Debates within Seventeenth-Century British Puritanism*. Reformed Historical Theology 17. Göttingen: Vandenhoeck & Ruprecht, 2011.

Holberton, Edward. *Poetry and the Cromwellian Protectorate: Culture, Politics, and Institutions*. Oxford: Oxford University Press, 2008.

Hopper, Andrew. *"Black Tom": Sir Thomas Fairfax and the English Revolution*. Politics, Culture, and Society in Early Modern Britain. Manchester: Manchester University Press, 2007.

Howson, Barry H. "The Puritan Hermeneutics of John Owen: A Recommendation." *Westminster Theological Journal* 63, no. 2 (2001): 351–76.

Hughes, Ann. "'The Public Confession of These Nations': The National Church in Interregnum England." In *Religion in Revolutionary England*, edited by Christopher Durston and Judith Maltby, 93–114. Manchester: Manchester University Press, 2006.

Hunsinger, George. "Justification and Mystical Union with Christ: Where Does Owen Stand?" In *The Ashgate Research Companion to John Owen's Theology*, edited by Kelly M. Kapic and Mark Jones, 199–214. Aldershot, UK: Ashgate, 2012.

Hutton, Ronald. *The British Republic, 1649–1660.* New York: Macmillan, 1990.

———. *The Restoration: A Political and Religious History of England and Wales, 1658–1667.* Oxford: Oxford University Press, 1985.

Hyde, Daniel R. "'The Fire That Kindleth All Our Sacrifices to God': Owen and the Work of the Holy Spirit in Prayer." In *The Ashgate Research Companion to John Owen's Theology,* edited by Kelly M. Kapic and Mark Jones, 249–70. Aldershot, UK: Ashgate, 2012.

Jacob, James R. *Henry Stubbe, Radical Protestantism and the Early Enlightenment.* Cambridge: Cambridge University Press, 1983.

Kapic, Kelly M. *Communion with God: The Divine and the Human in the Theology of John Owen.* Grand Rapids, MI: Baker Academic, 2007.

———. "Owen, John (1616–1683)." In *Dictionary of Major Biblical Interpreters,* edited by Donald K. McKim, 795–99. 2nd ed. Downers Grove, IL: IVP Academic, 2007.

———. "The Spirit as Gift: Explorations in John Owen's Pneumatology." In *The Ashgate Research Companion to John Owen's Theology,* edited by Kelly M. Kapic and Mark Jones, 113–40. Aldershot, UK: Ashgate, 2012.

———. "Typology, the Messiah, and John Owen's Theological Reading of Hebrews." In *Christology, Hermeneutics, and Hebrews: Profiles from the History of Interpretation,* edited by Jon C. Laansma and Daniel J. Treier, 135–54. Library of New Testament Studies 423. Edinburgh: T&T Clark, 2012.

Kay, Brian K. *Trinitarian Spirituality: John Owen and the Doctrine of God in Western Devotion.* Studies in Christian History and Thought. Milton Keynes, UK: Paternoster, 2007.

Keeble, N. H. "'But the Colonel's Shadow': Lucy Hutchinson, Women's Writing, and the Civil War." In *Literature and the En-*

glish Civil War, edited by Thomas Healy and Jonathan Sawday, 227–47. Cambridge: Cambridge University Press, 1990.

———. *The Literary Culture of Nonconformity in Later Seventeenth-Century England*. Leicester, UK: Leicester University Press, 1987.

Kelly, Ryan. "Reformed or Reforming? John Owen and the Complexity of Theological Codification for Mid-Seventeenth-Century England." In *The Ashgate Research Companion to John Owen's Theology*, edited by Kelly M. Kapic and Mark Jones, 3–30. Aldershot, UK: Ashgate, 2012.

Kelly, William. "Appendix to the Notice of the *Achill Herald* Recollections." *The Bible Treasury* 140 (1868): 14–15.

King, David M. "The Affective Spirituality of John Owen." *Evangelical Quarterly* 68, no. 3 (1996): 223–33.

Knapp, Henry M. "Augustine and Owen on Perseverance." *Westminster Theological Journal* 62, no. 1 (2000): 65–88.

———. "John Owen, on Schism and the Nature of the Church." *Westminster Theological Journal* 72 (2010): 333–58.

———. "John Owen's Interpretation of Hebrews 6:4–6: Eternal Perseverance of the Saints in Puritan Exegesis." *Calvin Theological Journal* 34, no. 1 (2003): 29–52.

Lake, Peter. *The Antichrist's Lewd Hat: Protestants, Papists and Players in Post-Reformation England*. With Michael Questier. New Haven, CT: Yale University Press, 2002.

———. *The Boxmaker's Revenge: "Orthodoxy," "Heterodoxy" and the Politics of the Parish in Early Stuart London*. Manchester: Manchester University Press, 2001.

———. "'A Charitable Christian Hatred': The Godly and Their Enemies in the 1630s." In *The Culture of English Puritanism, 1560–1700*, edited by Christopher Durston and Jacqueline Eales, 145–83. New York: Palgrave Macmillan, 1996.

Lake, Peter, and Steve Pincus. "Rethinking the Public Sphere in Early Modern England." *Journal of British Studies* 45, no. 2 (2006): 270–92.

Lee, Francis. *John Owen Re-Presbyterianized*. Edmonton, AB: Still Waters Revival, 2000.

Leggett, Donald. "John Owen as Religious Adviser to Oliver Cromwell, 1649–1659." MPhil thesis, University of Cambridge, 2006.

Letham, Robert. "John Owen's Doctrine of the Trinity in Its Catholic Context." In *The Ashgate Research Companion to John Owen's Theology*, edited by Kelly M. Kapic and Mark Jones, 185–98. Aldershot, UK: Ashgate, 2012.

———. *The Westminster Assembly: Reading Its Theology in Historical Context*. Phillipsburg, NJ: P&R, 2009.

Lim, Paul C.-H. *In Pursuit of Purity, Unity, and Liberty: Richard Baxter's Puritan Ecclesiology and Its Seventeenth-Century Context*. Leiden: Brill, 2004.

———. *Mystery Unveiled: The Crisis of the Trinity in Early Modern England*. Oxford Studies in Historical Theology. Oxford: Oxford University Press, 2012.

———. "Puritans and the Church of England: Historiography and Ecclesiology." In *The Cambridge Companion to Puritanism*, edited by John Coffey and Paul C.-H. Lim, 223–40. Cambridge: Cambridge University Press, 2008.

———. "The Trinity, *Adiaphora*, Ecclesiology, and Reformation: John Owen's Theory of Religious Toleration in Context." *Westminster Theological Journal* 67 (2005): 281–300.

Liu, Tai. *Discord in Zion: The Puritan Divines and the Puritan Revolution, 1640–1660*. The Hague, Netherlands: Martinus Nijhoff, 1973.

Lloyd, R. Glynne. *John Owen: Commonwealth Puritan*. Pontypridd, UK: Modern Welsh Publications, 1972.

MacFarlane, Alan. *The Family Life of Ralph Josselin: A Seventeenth-Century Clergyman*. New York: Norton, 1973.

Mayor, Stephen. "The Teaching of John Owen concerning the Lord's Supper." *Scottish Journal of Theology* 18, no. 2 (1965): 170–81.

McDonald, Suzanne. "Beholding the Glory of God in the Face of Jesus Christ: John Owen and the 'Reforming' of the Beatific Vision." In *The Ashgate Research Companion to John Owen's Theology*, edited by Kelly M. Kapic and Mark Jones, 141–58. Aldershot, UK: Ashgate, 2012.

———. "The Pneumatology of the 'Lost' Image in John Owen." *Westminster Theological Journal* 71, no. 2 (2009): 323–36.

McDowell, Nicholas. *Poetry and Allegiance in the English Civil Wars: Marvell and the Cause of Wit*. Oxford: Oxford University Press, 2008.

McGrath, Gavin J. "Puritans and the Human Will: Voluntarism within Mid-Seventeenth Century English Puritanism as Seen in the Works of Richard Baxter and John Owen." PhD diss., Durham University, 1989.

McGraw, Ryan M. *A Heavenly Directory: Trinitarian Piety, Public Worship and a Reassessment of John Owen's Theology*. Bristol, CT: Vandenhoeck & Ruprecht, 2014.

———. "John Owen on the Holy Spirit in Relation to the Trinity, the Humanity of Christ, and the Believer." In *The Beauty and Glory of the Holy Spirit*, edited by Joel R. Beeke and Joseph A. Pipa, 267–84. Grand Rapids, MI: Reformation Heritage Books, 2012.

———. *John Owen: Trajectories in Reformed Orthodox Theology*. Cham, Switzerland: Palgrave Macmillan, 2017.

McKim, Donald K. "John Owen's Doctrine of Scripture in Historical Perspective." *Evangelical Quarterly* 45 (1973): 195–207.

McKinley, David J. "John Owen's View of Illumination: An Alternative to the Fuller-Erickson Dialogue." *Bibliotheca Sacra* 154 (1997): 93–104.

McLaughlin, Gráinne. "The Idolater John Owen? Linguistic Hegemony in Cromwell's Oxford." In *Scholarly Self-Fashioning and Community in the Early Modern University*, edited by Richard Kirwan, 145–66. Farnham, UK: Ashgate, 2013.

Miller, Peter N. "The 'Antiquarianization' of Biblical Scholarship and the London Polyglot Bible (1653–57)." *Journal of the History of Ideas* 62, no. 3 (2001): 463–82.

Milton, Anthony. *Catholic and Reformed: The Roman and Protestant Churches in English Protestant Thought, 1600–1640.* Cambridge Studies in Early Modern British History. Cambridge: Cambridge University Press, 1995.

Moffatt, James, ed. *The Golden Book of John Owen: Passages from the Writings of the Rev. John Owen.* London: Hodder and Stoughton, 1904.

Morrill, John. "The Church of England, 1642–1649." In *The Nature of the English Revolution*, 148–76. Harlow, UK: Routledge, 1993.

Morrill, John, and Philip Baker. "Oliver Cromwell, the Regicide and the Sons of Zeruiah." In *Cromwell and the Interregnum*, edited by David L. Smith, 15–36. Blackwell Essential Readings in History. Oxford: Blackwell, 2003.

Mortimer, Sarah. *Reason and Religion in the English Revolution: The Challenge of Socinianism.* Cambridge Studies in Early Modern British History. Cambridge: Cambridge University Press, 2010.

Muller, Richard A. *After Calvin: Studies in the Development of a Theological Tradition.* Oxford Studies in Historical Theology. Oxford: Oxford University Press, 2003.

———. "Directions in the Study of Early Modern Reformed Thought." *Perichoresis* 14, no. 3 (2016): 3–16.

———. *Post-Reformation Reformed Dogmatics: The Rise and Development of Reformed Orthodoxy, ca. 1520 to ca. 1725.* 4 vols. Grand Rapids, MI: Baker, 2003.

———. "Reflections on Persistent Whiggism and Its Antidotes in the Study of Sixteenth- and Seventeenth-Century Intellectual History." In *Seeing Things Their Way: Intellectual History and the Return of Religion*, edited by Alister Chapman, John Coffey, and Brad S. Gregory, 134–53. South Bend, IN: University of Notre Dame Press, 2009.

Najapfour, Brian G. "'That It Might Lead and Direct Men unto Christ': John Owen's View of the Mosaic Covenant." *Scottish Bulletin of Evangelical Theology* 29, no. 2 (2011): 196–204.

Narveson, Katherine. "The Sources for Lucy Hutchinson's *On Theology*," *Notes and Queries*, n.s., 36 (1989): 40–41.

Norbrook, David. *Writing the English Republic: Poetry, Rhetoric and Politics, 1627–1660*. Cambridge: Cambridge University Press, 1999.

Nuttall, Geoffrey F. "Milton's Churchmanship in 1659: His Letter to Jean de Labadie." *Milton Quarterly* 35, no. 4 (2001): 227–31.

O'Donnell, Laurence R., III. "The Holy Spirit's Role in John Owen's 'Covenant of the Mediator' Formulation: A Case Study in Reformed Orthodox Formulations of the *Pactum Salutis*." *Puritan Reformed Journal* 4, no. 1 (2012): 91–115.

Oliver, Robert W. "John Owen: His Life and Times." In *John Owen: The Man and His Theology*, edited by Robert W. Oliver, 9–40. Phillipsburg, NJ: P&R, 2002.

———, ed. *John Owen: The Man and His Theology*. Phillipsburg, NJ: P&R, 2002.

Patterson, Annabel, and Martin Dzelzainis. "Marvell and the Earl of Anglesey: A Chapter in the History of Reading." *Historical Journal* 44, no. 3 (2001): 703–26.

Patterson, W. B. *William Perkins and the Making of a Protestant England*. Oxford: Oxford University Press, 2014.

Payne, Jon D. *John Owen on the Lord's Supper*. Edinburgh: Banner of Truth, 2004.

Pederson, Randall J. "Reformed Orthodoxy in Puritanism." *Perichoresis* 14, no. 3 (2016): 45–59.

Pettegree, Andrew. *Reformation and the Culture of Persuasion*. Cambridge: Cambridge University Press, 2005.

Piper, John. *Contending for Our All: Defending Truth and Treasuring Christ in the Lives of Athanasius, John Owen, and J. Gresham Machen.* Wheaton, IL: Crossway, 2006.

Polizzotto, Carolyn. "The Campaign against *The Humble Proposals* of 1652." *Journal of Ecclesiastical History* 38 (1987): 569–81.

Powell, Hunter. *The Crisis of British Protestantism: Church Power in the Puritan Revolution, 1638–44.* Politics, Culture, and Society in Early Modern Britain. Manchester: Manchester University Press, 2015.

Powicke, F. J. "Dr. Lewis Du Moulin's Vindication of the Congregational Way." *Congregational Historical Society Transactions* 9 (1924–1926): 219–36.

Rehnman, Sebastian. *Divine Discourse: The Theological Methodology of John Owen.* Texts and Studies in Reformation and Post-Reformation Thought. Grand Rapids, MI: Baker Academic, 2002.

———. "John Owen: A Reformed Scholastic at Oxford." In *Reformation and Scholasticism: An Ecumenical Enterprise*, edited by Willem J. van Asselt and Eef Dekker, 181–203. Texts and Studies in Reformation and Post-Reformation Thought. Grand Rapids, MI: Baker Academic, 2001.

———. "John Owen on Faith and Reason." In *The Ashgate Research Companion to John Owen's Theology*, edited by Kelly M. Kapic and Mark Jones, 31–48. Aldershot, UK: Ashgate, 2012.

Ryrie, Alec. *Being Protestant in Reformation Britain.* Oxford: Oxford University Press, 2013.

Ryrie, Alec, and Tom Schwanda, eds. *Puritanism and Emotion in the Early Modern World.* Christianities in the Trans-Atlantic World, 1500–1800. Basingstoke, UK: Palgrave Macmillan, 2016.

Seaward, Paul. *The Cavalier Parliament and the Reconstruction of the Old Regime, 1661–1667.* Cambridge Studies in Early

Modern British History. Cambridge: Cambridge University Press, 1989.

Sharpe, Kevin. *Reading Revolutions: The Politics of Reading in Early Modern England*. New Haven, CT: Yale University Press, 2000.

Shaw, William A. *A History of the English Church during the Civil Wars and under the Commonwealth, 1640–1660*. 2 vols. London: Longmans, Green, 1900.

Simonutti, Luisa. "Political Society and Religious Liberty: Locke at Cleves and in Holland." *British Journal for the History of Philosophy* 14, no. 3 (2006): 413–36.

Skinner, Quentin. *Reason and Rhetoric in the Philosophy of Hobbes*. Cambridge: Cambridge University Press, 1996.

———. *Visions of Politics*. Vol. 1, *Regarding Method*. Cambridge: Cambridge University Press, 2002.

Slack, Paul. *The Impact of Plague in Tudor and Stuart England*. Oxford: Oxford University Press, 1995.

Smith, Christopher R. "'Up and Be Doing': The Pragmatic Puritan Eschatology of John Owen." *Evangelical Quarterly* 61 (1989): 335–49.

Smith, Nigel. *Literature and Revolution in England, 1640–1660*. New Haven, CT: Yale University Press, 1994.

Snoddy, Richard. "A Display of Learning? Citations and Shortcuts in John Owen's *A Display of Arminianisme* (1643)." *Westminster Theological Journal* (forthcoming).

Spence, Alan. "Christ's Humanity and Ours: John Owen." In *Persons, Divine and Human*, edited by Christoph Schwöbel and Colin E. Gunton, 74–97. Edinburgh: T&T Clark, 1991.

———. *Incarnation and Inspiration: John Owen and the Coherence of Christology*. T&T Clark Theology. London: T&T Clark, 2007.

———. "John Owen and Trinitarian Agency." *Scottish Journal of Theology* 43, no. 2 (1990): 157–73.

———. "The Significance of John Owen for Modern Christology." In *The Ashgate Research Companion to John Owen's Theology*, edited by Kelly M. Kapic and Mark Jones, 171–84. Aldershot, UK: Ashgate, 2012.

Spufford, Margaret. *Contrasting Communities: English Villagers in the Sixteenth and Seventeenth Centuries*. Cambridge: Cambridge University Press, 1974.

Spurlock, R. Scott. *Cromwell and Scotland: Conquest and Religion, 1650–1660*. Edinburgh: John Donald, 2007.

Spurr, John. *The Restoration Church of England, 1646–1689*. New Haven, CT: Yale University Press, 1991.

Stachniewski, John. *The Persecutory Imagination: English Puritanism and the Literature of Religious Despair*. Oxford: Clarendon, 1991.

Stevenson, Jane. "Introduction." In *The Works of Lucy Hutchinson*, edited by Elizabeth Clarke, David Norbrook, and Jane Stevenson, with textual introductions by Jonathan Gibson and editorial assistance from Mark Burden and Alice Eardley. Oxford: Oxford University Press, 2018.

Svensson, Manfred. "John Owen and John Locke: Confessionalism, Doctrinal Minimalism, and Toleration." *History of European Ideas* 43, no. 4 (2017): 302–16.

Tay, Edwin E. M. "Christ's Priestly Oblation and Intercession: Their Development and Significance in John Owen." In *The Ashgate Research Companion to John Owen's Theology*, edited by Kelly M. Kapic and Mark Jones, 159–69. Aldershot, UK: Ashgate, 2012.

———. *The Priesthood of Christ: Atonement in the Theology of John Owen (1616–1683)*. Studies in Christian History and Thought. Milton Keynes, UK: Paternoster, 2014.

Toon, Peter. *God's Statesman: The Life and Work of John Owen*. Exeter, UK: Paternoster, 1971.

Troxel, A. Craig. "'Cleansed Once for All': John Owen on the Glory of Gospel Worship in Hebrews." *Calvin Theological Journal* 32 (1997): 468–79.

Trueman, Carl R. *The Claims of Truth: John Owen's Trinitarian Theology*. Carlisle, UK: Paternoster, 1998.

———. "Faith Seeking Understanding: Some Neglected Aspects of John Owen's Understanding of Scriptural Interpretation." In *Interpreting the Bible: Historical and Theological Studies in Honour of David F. Wright*, edited by A. N. S. Lane, 147–62. Leicester, UK: Apollos, 1997.

———. "John Owen as a Theologian." In *John Owen: The Man and His Theology*, edited by Robert W. Oliver, 41–68. Phillipsburg, NJ: P&R, 2002.

———. *John Owen: Reformed Catholic, Renaissance Man*. Great Theologians. Aldershot, UK: Ashgate, 2007.

Trueman, Carl R., and R. Scott Clark, eds. *Protestant Scholasticism: Essays in Reassessment*. Studies in Christian History and Thought. Carlisle, UK: Paternoster, 1999.

Tweeddale, John W. *John Owen and Hebrews: The Foundation of Biblical Interpretation*. T&T Clark Studies in English Theology. London: T&T Clark, 2019.

———. "A John Owen Bibliography." In *The Ashgate Research Companion to John Owen's Theology*, edited by Kelly M. Kapic and Mark Jones, 297–328. Aldershot, UK: Ashgate, 2012.

———. "John Owen's Commentary on Hebrews in Context." In *The Ashgate Research Companion to John Owen's Theology*, edited by Kelly M. Kapic and Mark Jones, 49–64. Aldershot, UK: Ashgate, 2012.

Tyacke, Nicholas. *Aspects of English Protestantism, c. 1530–1700*. Politics, Culture, and Society in Early Modern Britain. Manchester: Manchester University Press, 2001.

Underdown, David. *Royalist Conspiracy in England, 1649–1660*. New Haven, CT: Yale University Press, 1971.

van Asselt, Willem J. "Covenant Theology as Relational Theology: The Contributions of Johannes Cocceius (1603–1669) and John Owen (1618–1683) to a Living Reformed Theology." In

The Ashgate Research Companion to John Owen's Theology, edited by Kelly M. Kapic and Mark Jones, 65–84. Aldershot, UK: Ashgate, 2012.

———. Introduction to Reformed Scholasticism. Translated by Albert Gootjes. Grand Rapids, MI: Reformation Heritage Books, 2011.

Van Biema, David. "10 Ideas Changing the World Right Now: The New Calvinism." Time, March 12, 2009.

van den Brink, Gert. "Impetration and Application in John Owen's Theology." In The Ashgate Research Companion to John Owen's Theology, edited by Kelly M. Kapic and Mark Jones, 85–96. Aldershot, UK: Ashgate, 2012.

VanDrunen, David. Natural Law and the Two Kingdoms: A Study in the Development of Reformed Social Thought. Emory University Studies in Law and Religion. Grand Rapids, MI: Eerdmans, 2009.

Vernon, Elliot. "The Quarrel of the Covenant: The London Presbyterians and the Regicide." In The Regicides and the Execution of Charles I, edited by Jason Peacey, 202–24. New York: Palgrave Macmillan, 2001.

Wallace, Dewey D. "Owen, John (1616–1683)." In Puritans and Puritanism in Europe and America: A Comprehensive Encyclopedia, edited by Francis J. Bremer and Tom Webster, 187–89. Santa Barbara, CA: ABC-CLIO, 2006.

———. Puritans and Predestination: Grace in English Protestant Theology, 1525–1695. Studies in Religion. Chapel Hill: University of North Carolina Press, 1982.

———. Shapers of English Calvinism, 1660–1714: Variety, Persistence, and Transformation. Oxford Studies in Historical Theology. Oxford: Oxford University Press, 2011.

Walsham, Alexandra. Providence in Early Modern England. Oxford: Oxford University Press, 1999.

Ward, W. R. Early Evangelicalism: A Global Intellectual History, 1670–1789. Cambridge: Cambridge University Press, 2006.

Watkins, Owen C. *The Puritan Experience: Studies in Spiritual Autobiography.* London: Routledge and Kegan Paul, 1972.

Watt, Tessa. *Cheap Print and Popular Piety, 1550–1640.* Cambridge Studies in Early Modern British History. Cambridge: Cambridge University Press, 1991.

Webster, Tom. "Early Stuart Puritanism." In *The Cambridge Companion to Puritanism*, edited by John Coffey and Paul C.-H. Lim, 48–66. Cambridge: Cambridge University Press, 2008.

———. *Godly Clergy in Early Stuart England: The Caroline Puritan Movement, c. 1620–1643.* Cambridge Studies in Early Modern British History. Cambridge: Cambridge University Press, 1997.

Westcott, Stephen P. *By the Bible Alone! John Owen's Puritan Theology for Today's Church.* Fellsmere, FL: Reformation Media & Press, 2010.

Wilken, Robert Louis. *Liberty in the Things of God: The Christian Origins of Religious Freedom.* New Haven, CT: Yale University Press, 2019.

Wilson, John F. *Pulpit in Parliament: Puritanism during the English Civil Wars, 1640–1648.* Princeton, NJ: Princeton University Press, 1969.

Wilson, Peter H. *The Thirty Years War: Europe's Tragedy.* Cambridge, MA: Belknap Press of Harvard University Press, 2009.

Wood, Anthony à. *Athenae Oxonienses.* 4 vols. Oxford, 1813.

Woolhouse, Roger. *Locke: A Biography.* Cambridge: Cambridge University Press, 2007.

Woolrych, Austin. *Britain in Revolution, 1625–1660.* Oxford: Oxford University Press, 2002.

———. *Commonwealth to Protectorate.* Oxford: Clarendon, 1982.

Worden, Blair. *Literature and Politics in Cromwellian England: John Milton, Andrew Marvell, Marchamont Nedham.* Oxford: Oxford University Press, 2007.

————. "Oliver Cromwell and the Sin of Achan." In *Cromwell and the Interregnum*, edited by David L. Smith, 37–59. Blackwell Essential Readings in History. Oxford: Blackwell, 2003.

————. "Politics, Piety, and Learning: Cromwellian Oxford." Chap. 4 in *God's Instruments: Political Conduct in the England of Oliver Cromwell*. Oxford: Oxford University Press, 2012.

Wrightson, Keith, and David Levine. *Poverty and Piety in an English Village: Terling, 1525–1700*. Rev. ed. Oxford: Oxford University Press, 1995.

Yule, George. *The Independents in the English Civil War*. Cambridge: Cambridge University Press, 1958.

General Index

Act of Oblivion (1660), 91, 100
Act of Uniformity (1662), 128
adoption, 63, 66
  and baptism, 53
affections, 75–76, 89
Aldersey, Thomas, 79–80, 81
American Revolution, 115, 149
Anabaptists, 52
angels, 135
antichrist, 125, 128
Apostles' Creed, 60, 63, 65, 68
Aristotle, 73, 78
Arminianism, 30
assurance of salvation, 32, 145
Augustine, 129, 152

Baillie, Robert, 92
Banner of Truth, 40, 151
baptism, 34, 43, 51–59, 66
  as beginning of Christian forma-
    tion, 47, 52, 59
  of children of believers, 47
  and church membership, 56
  and regeneration of infants, 53
  removes inherent lust and pollu-
    tion, 53
  as sign and seal, 54, 55, 57, 59
  and spiritual nurture of children,
    51

Baptists, 34
Baxter, Richard, 26, 145
bearing the cross, 138
beatific vision, 118, 119, 138, 146
being "with Christ" in death, 136
biographical theology, 14
Blasphemy Act (1648), 34
Book of Common Prayer, 61
*Brief Instruction in the Worship of
    God, A* (1667), 57, 94, 105,
    109, 110
Brownists, 49
Bunyan, John, 25, 98
Burgess, Cornelius, 53
busyness, 27

Calvin, John, 152
  Institutes, 82–83, 90
  on word and sacrament, 109
Caryl, Joseph, 39, 112
catechesis, 43
  in early church, 57
  nurtured spiritual life, 68
catechism in *The Primer*, 63–64, 65
catechisms in *The Principles of the
    Doctrine of Christ*, 48, 51,
    65–68
Catholics, on baptism, 52

Charles I, King, execution of, 35, 120, 124, 131
Charles II, King, 26, 38, 96, 110, 130, 140
Chaucer, Geoffrey, 25
childhood, 43, 47–69
child mortality, 49–50
child-rearing, 49–51
Christian formation, 59–65
  begins with baptism, 47, 52, 59
Christian home, 48
Christian liberty, 66
Christian life, 13–14
  proceeds from grace to grace, 152–53
  vicissitudes of, 91
  See also spiritual life
Christian pilgrimage, 148
church, marks of, 51
Church of England, worship in, 105
church membership, 43, 62
  not at baptism, 52, 56, 58
church order, 110
church-state relations, 99, 102, 148, 152
civil war, 119
Clarendon Code (1661–1665), 92, 94, 98
classical liberalism, 95, 100–101, 147–49, 152
Coggeshall, 33
Colchester, 35
communion with Christ, 44
communion with the triune God, 80–81, 82–83
Congregationalists, 33, 109
congregational life, 105–6
Constantinian politics, 102, 148
Cooper, Tim, 42, 145
Cowan, Martyn, 42
Cromwell, Oliver, 25, 35–37, 97, 126, 140, 150

church settlement under, 57
death of, 37
Cromwell, Richard, 37

Dante Alighieri, 25
death, 44, 131–36
  facing with confidence, 117
  preparing for, 134–35
Declaration of Indulgence (1672), 110
despair, literature of, 145
Directory for Public Worship (Westminster Assembly), 54, 61
Discourse concerning Christian Love and Peace (1672), 108
Display of Arminianism (1643), 32
dissent, 128, 130
dissenters, 26, 137
  ecclesiastical censures of, 98
  not revolutionary, 99
  in public life, 97–100
Donatists, 56
Dormer, Robert, 30–31
Du Moulin, Lewis, 114
dying in faith, 134–35

Earl of Clarendon, 94
Earl of Oxford, 26
education, as restorative, 79
elders, 110–11
Eliot, Jim, 40
"empty professors," 74–75
endurance, 111
English Civil Wars, 26, 30, 35–36, 52
  and closing chapters of Revelation, 123
  providential reading of, 130
English Reformation
  final reversal of, 140
  weakness in program of confessionalization, 67
English Revolution, 35

Enlightenment, 43
eschatology, 119–31
evangelicalism, 149–52
ex opere operato, 53
extemporaneous worship, 61–62

Fairfax, Thomas, 35
fall, 78
false worship, 107
Father
　as "fountain of the Deity," 85–86
　love for believers, 85–87
final glory, 44
first catechism (1645), 53
First Tract on Government (Locke),
　96
Fleetwood, Charles, 139–40
Fleetwood, Cromwell, 114
Fletcher, Giles, 127
Fordham, Essex parish, 33
fountain imagery, 85–88

Gale, Theophilus, 128
Geneva Bible, 125
globalization of Protestant Christi-
　anity, 119–23
Glorious Revolution, 40, 95, 149
God
　as Father, 62–63, 68
　sovereignty of, 85, 93–94
Goodwin, John, 92
Goodwin, Thomas, 92, 122
Goold, William H., 23, 40
grace, 13, 152
"greater catechism" of Owen,
　67–68
Great Fire of London (1666), 38,
　44, 107, 119, 128
Great Plague (1665–1666), 38, 44,
　107, 129

Hartlib, Samuel, 77
Hartopp, Elizabeth, 132–33

Hartopp, John, 109
Hebrews, Owen's commentary on,
　25, 111, 150
Herbert, John Rogers, 150
Holy Spirit
　person and work of, 148
　and public worship, 61
　as well of water springing up in
　　the soul, 87
Homer, 73
human flourishing, 145
Hutchinson, John, 114
Hutchinson, Lucy, 26, 109, 114
Hyde, Edward, 93
hypocrites, 75

idolatry, 108
Independent church order, 38
individual experience, 149–50
individual spirituality, 152
infant baptism, 47, 58
　rejection of, 55–56
instruction in the faith, 43
intermediate state, 44, 117–18, 134
Ireland, invasion of, 35, 41
Israel, future of biblical land,
　127–28

James I, King, 29
James II, King (also Duke of York),
　26, 39–40, 110, 130, 140
Jefferson, Thomas, 115
Jesus Christ
　as fountain of grace and mercy,
　　86
　glory of, 137–38
　second coming of, 118
Jews, latter-day conversion of,
　125–27
Johnston, Archibald, 35
Jonson, Ben, 84
Josselin, Ralph, 33–34, 50
justification, 63, 147

Kelly, William, 40
knowing the times, 120, 130
knowledge of God and ourselves, 83, 90

Laud, William, 73
Laudianism, 105
law of nature, 101–2
Lee, Samuel, 127
"lesser catechism" of Owen, 65–66, 68
liberty, 149
liberty of conscience, 96, 104
liberty of worship, 130
Lloyd-Jones, D. Martyn, 40, 151
Locke, John, 78, 95–96, 99, 101, 104, 147, 148–49, 152
London, 31
Lord's Prayer, 60–63, 65, 68
    use by children, 62
Lord's Supper, 34, 66
    restricted admission to, 67
    weekly observance of, 109, 113
Louis XIV, King, of France, 130
Lovelace, John, 31
Lovelace, Richard, 31

Manasseh ben Israel, 126
Marvell, Andrew, 25
Meditations and Discourses on the Glory of Christ (1684), 119, 137
middle life, 115–16
millennial theory, 121–22
Milton, John, 26, 77, 92, 150
missionary expansion, 124
mortality, 118
mortification, 80, 136
Muller, Richard A., 41

new Calvinism, 151
"New Confession of Faith, A" (1654), 55

new covenant, 108
New Testament, on worship, 107
nonconformity
    not a threat to government, 99
    and public peace and tranquility, 103
Nye, Philip, 37

Of Communion with God (1657), 36, 81, 82–85, 143
Of the Mortification of Sin in Believers (1656), 36, 80
overbusy life, 27
Owen, Henry (father), 48
Owen, John
    abandoned scholastic approach, 71, 72, 79, 82
    ambiguous defense of infant baptism, 58
    as "Atlas of the Independents," 93
    changing homiletical practice, 134
    conversion of, 74
    dean of Christ Church, 36, 41, 76, 78
    death of, 139–41
    deaths of his children, 44, 131, 132
    depression, 31, 39, 71
    diligent in studies, 73
    ecclesiology of, 150
    election as an MP, 37
    evolving doctrine of baptism, 52–56
    on grace, 152
    library of, 73
    nontheological interests of, 144
    Oxford education, 73–74
    in painting of Westminster Assembly, 150
    as parish minister, 26, 33
    pastored congregation in Wallingford House, 37
    political theory of, 100–101

preaching to Oxford undergraduates, 72
on religious toleration, 95–104
as "sincere friend of liberty," 116
vice-chancellor of Oxford, 36, 41,
76, 91, 131
Owen, Mary (wife), 33, 49
death of, 39, 133
Oxford University, 29–30. *See* University of Oxford

peaceable kingdom, 128
*Peace Offering, or an Apology and
Humble Plea for Indulgence
and Liberty of Conscience, A*
(1667), 97
Perrinchief, Richard, 104
perseverance, 88, 153
Pink, A. W., 40
Plato, 78
Polhill, Mrs. Edward, 133
poor and needy, 95
post-Constantinian politics, 148
prayers for children, 155–57
Presbyterians, rise and fall in English
Civil Wars, 52, 67
preterism, 122
Primer (1652), 48, 59–64, 68,
155–57
*Principles of the Doctrine of Christ,
Unfolded in Two Short Catechisms* (1645), 65, 68
private worship, 60–61
progressive sanctification, 153
providential interpretation of history, 130
public worship, 60–61
"pure milk of the word," 69
Puritans
emotional life of, 145
on eschatology, 119–20
ridicule of, 49

Queen's College, Oxford, 29–30, 73

rebaptism, 56
Reformed confessions, Constantinian politics of, 148
regicide, 35, 92, 119, 120
religious toleration, 25, 95–104,
148–49, 152
religious uniformity, 102
resistance to government, 103
Restoration, 26, 57, 91–93, 96, 116,
119
evils of, 129, 131
political theory of, 43
resurrection, 44, 66, 138–39
Reynolds, Edward, 79–80
ritualism, and natural disasters, 107
Roman Empire, as fourth beast of
Revelation, 124
Rooke, Mary. *See* Owen, Mary
(wife)
Rush, Benjamin, 115
Ryrie, Alec, 145

sacramental efficacy, 55
sacraments, 51
saints, grow in grace, 74–75
Sams, John, 34
sanctification, 63, 153
Satan, binding of, 129
Savoy Declaration (1658), 57, 105,
106, 125
scholastic theology, 71, 72, 79, 82
Schwanda, Tom, 145
Scientific Revolution, 43
Scotland, invasion of, 35, 41
Scudder, Henry, 71–72, 75, 79, 88,
90
second baptism, 56
seeing Christ "face to face," 138–39
sermon gadding, 114
set prayers, 60, 64
Shakespeare, William, 84

sin, separation from, 136
Socinianism, 82
Socrates, 78
spiritual experience, 85, 149–50
spiritual life, 13, 43–45
    begun in childhood, 43
    clarified by dying, 132
    joyful possibilities of, 146
    as quiet life, 100, 115
    sustained by grace, 28
    and toleration, 148
spiritual nurture, 51, 58, 68
Stachniewski, John, 144–45
Stadhampton, 48–49
Steele, William, 135
Stubbe, Henry, 27, 95–96
suffering, 138
superstition, 134

Ten Commandments, 60, 63, 65, 68
Test Act (1673), 110
Theologoumena Pantodapa (1661),
    114
Thirty-Nine Articles, 38, 106
Thirty Years' War, 124
Thomas Aquinas, 118, 152
Thorseby, Ralph, 114
time management, 27
total depravity, 88
Trinity, communion with, 80

*True Nature of a Gospel Church,
    The* (1689), 81
Two Treatises of Government
    (Locke), 101, 147

unconditional election, 88
union with Christ, 66
Unitarians, 40, 149
University of Oxford, 26, 29–30,
    41, 59, 91, 131

Vindiciae Evangelicae (1655), 82

Walker, Robert, 131
walking with God, 72, 75, 77, 90
Wallingford House, 37
Watts, Isaac, 40, 149
Wesley, John, 40, 150
Westminster Assembly, 33, 34
Westminster Shorter Catechism, 63
Whig literary culture, 97
Wilkins, John, 79
Wilkinson, Henry (Christ Church),
    79
Wilkinson, Henry (Magdalene Col-
    lege), 79
William of Orange, 40
Works of John Owen, 23, 40
worship, 60–61, 105–9

"young, restless, and Reformed"
    movement, 151

Scripture Index

1 Samuel
1:8 133

Job
book of. 39

Psalms
84:11 153
90:10 139
104 64
130 58

Jeremiah
22:16 95

Daniel
book of. 124

Zephaniah
3:17. 86

Zechariah
13:1. 85

Matthew
2 64
24. 122

John
1:16. 152–53
17:24 137

18–19. 64
21:20 81

Acts
3:21. 121
14:23 111

Romans
8:13. 80
8:28. 94
11:36 15

1 Corinthians
7:14. 58
11:24 113
13:13 135
15:31 134

2 Corinthians
4:6 118
13:14 80

Ephesians
4:8 111
4:14–15 69

Philippians
3:20. 148

1 Thessalonians
4:11. 115

2 Thessalonians
1:10.................139
3:12.................115

1 Timothy
2:2..................115

Hebrews
book of............25, 111, 126,
                    150
11:13 134
12:14 111

1 Peter
1:17................148
2:2 69

1 John
1:3 81
4:8 85

Revelation
book of............123
3:20................84
6 122
20..................129